CROSSCURRENTS *Modern Critiques*

CROSSCURRENTS *Modern Critiques*
Harry T. Moore, *General Editor*

James D. Brophy

Edith Sitwell

THE SYMBOLIST ORDER

WITH A PREFACE BY

Harry T. Moore

Carbondale and Edwardsville

SOUTHERN ILLINOIS UNIVERSITY PRESS

FEFFER & SIMONS, INC.

London and Amsterdam

To Betty

PREFACE

EDITH SITWELL was a spectacular figure and a remarkable poet. You could turn these phrases around and still "catch" her: a remarkable figure and a spectacular poet. As James D. Brophy points out in the present book, Dame Edith—and how she insisted upon her title!—has recently been somewhat neglected as a poet. This volume may help to bring an end to that situation, for the book is a thorough examination not only of Edith Sitwell's verse but also of her critical ideas.

Mr. Brophy begins with a long discussion of Edith Sitwell as a controversialist and critic. No one before him has dealt so thoroughly with all her critical writings, and his treatment of them makes a valuable prelude to his explication of the poetry.

Edith Sitwell has always had at least a minority of admirers, among them Stephen Spender and Sir Maurice Bowra. But her aggressiveness gained her many enemies, and her eccentricity put off a great number of potential admirers, who probably felt, with F. R. Leavis, that Edith Sitwell belonged more to the history of publicity than to poetry. (She slapped back at Leavis at every opportunity and even made opportunities for that particular activity.)

Her poetry recitals, often in company with her brother Sir Osbert, were plangently theatrical. The hawklike woman read her verse in a bardic chant, and the effect was electrifying, though the professional critics were not always won over.

But when we consider the poems seriously, in company with Mr. Brophy, we may be able to see what Dame Edith's minority of admirers find in them that is good. As his subtitle, The Symbolic Order, indicates, he investigates her as a symbolist, viewing her work partly in terms of her own symbolic use of the word shadow. But he also finds that she has affinities with the seventeenth-century metaphysicals. In effect, Mr. Brophy places Edith Sitwell in the continuing tradition of English and modern European poetry; but he also emphasizes her individuality.

In accomplishing this, he is admirably technical. Not that he doesn't examine ideas thoroughly; he also emphasizes craftsmanship. Too much of our literary criticism deals exclusively with ideas and avoids textures. Mr. Brophy has, in Edith Sitwell, a rich subject for technical discussion, and he makes the most of it. He gives us a valuable examination of a controversial and significant poet.

HARRY T. MOORE

Southern Illinois University
October 12, 1967

ACKNOWLEDGMENTS

I AM ESPECIALLY indebted to William York Tindall who read my work in progress and whose interest in my conception of Edith Sitwell's poetry encouraged me to write this book. Other readers who also offered perceptive criticism which I have endeavored to heed are Edward Tayler, John Unterecker, Leon Roudiez, and Robert Maguire. I remember with gratitude James Clifford and Brother Charles Quinn who, knowing I was working on Edith Sitwell, thoughtfully forwarded pertinent articles from English periodicals.

In the course of writing this book I have used a number of libraries, principally those of Columbia University and Iona and Sarah Lawrence Colleges. I thank the librarians of those institutions, particularly Miss Lillian Viacava of Iona, for much competent assistance.

Although I despair of ascertaining all that I owe, especially to teachers, colleagues, and friends, for whatever I know of my subject, I do know without qualification that my greatest debt is recognized in my dedication. But even that I shall not attempt to explain: in the words of him who wrote the greatest love poems in the language (according to Edith Sitwell)

> 'Twere profanation of our joys
> To tell the laity our love.

I am pleased to acknowledge the generous cooperation of Dame Edith Sitwell's heirs and publishers in allowing me to quote widely from the following editions of her poetry and prose: the *Collected Poems* and *Music and Ceremonies* (The Vanguard Press), *Alexander Pope* (W. W. Norton & Co., Inc.), *Poetry and Criticism* (Henry Holt and Company), and *Aspects of Modern Poetry* (Gerald Duckworth & Co., Ltd.).

The passages from Sir George Sitwell's *On the Making of Gardens* are used with the permission of Gerald Duckworth & Co., Ltd. Quotations from Reuben Brower's *The Fields of Light* are used with the permission of the Oxford University Press.

J. D. B.

CONTENTS

INTRODUCTION

VIGOROUS CONTROVERSY has played about Edith Sitwell
from the outset of her career in 1915, and even after her
death in 1964 articulate factions of those who worship and
those who cannot abide her continue to thrive. Perhaps no
other poet of our era—even Ezra Pound—has caused such
enduring partisan engagement. On one hand Stephen
Spender affirms that her imagery "is true to a very real
experience," [1] while on the other Geoffrey Grigson denounces her images as "monstrosities" and "untruths to
nature." [2] Yeats praises her "metrical virtuosity," [3] and
C. M. Bowra remarks the "great flowering of her genius." [4]
Two other critics, however, announce that they consider
her "to be no poet at all." [5]

Yet the scores of antipodal critics appear to concur in
recognizing that Edith Sitwell is a woman of extraordinary
individualism. This quality appears to be one basis, perhaps the central one, of both the eulogy and rejection of
Dame Edith: at one pole of taste she is praised for what is
regarded as genius; at the other, she is censured for exas-
perating caprice. Yeats, for example, in admiration speaks
of her "temperament of a strangeness so high-pitched that
only through . . . [powerful artificial vividness] could it
find expression." [6] Bowra calls her a "seer" and "a
prophet"; [7] Spender, also in approbation, emphasizes this
facet of personal uniqueness in citing her "rare and aristocratic quality" in "a poetry which no one except Miss
Sitwell could have written." [8]

These views—to the point of recognizing a *unique* personality—are shared by her detractors. We find, for instance, among the unsympathetic reviews of *Wheels* (the annual anthology of poetry which Edith Sitwell edited from 1916 through 1921) remarks such as "Mr. Osbert and Miss Edith Sitwell we can imagine as anxiously asking themselves: 'What can we do to be original' " [9] and "conceived in morbid eccentricity." [10] Such opinions appear to be confirmed by F. R. Leavis' famous remark that Edith Sitwell "belongs to the history of publicity rather than of poetry." [11] Her special eccentricity, a kind of aggressive isolation, has even been satirized in S. J. Perelman's Broadway comedy, *The Beauty Part*.[12]

The personal nature of the criticism which emanates from these extremes of praise and rejection of Sitwell's individualism is characterized by many anecdotes which aggrandize her extraordinary temperament. A well-known one describes a solicitous visitor asking the five-year-old Edith, "What do you want to be when you grow up?" The forthright response was an unequivocal, "A Genius." In relating this incident, her brother Osbert fittingly describes the little girl as "standing alone, with a singular isolation," and he further adds that his parents were indeed "rankled." [13] The anecdote is instructive, for not only does it inform us of Edith's early beginnings in provocation, but it also reveals something about our reactions to her. It is hard to imagine an "objective" response to this incident: either we consider the answer strikingly appropriate or insufferably brash. Any study, including this one, which attempts a disinterested approach must nonetheless be aware of the justification of the single response. Most of the anecdotes, like the one above, can be used without change (except in tone) for either disapprobation or praise—as is the case with the title "Queen Edith" bestowed on her by her friends. The deciding factor is the predisposition of those who are discussing Dame Edith.

The undeniable singularity of the poet's temperament and appearance encourages a reaction which characterizes her work as essentially imbued with intuition, a sign either of caprice or genius depending on the observer's point of view. It is further evident that some of this kind of analysis—or more accurately, impression—of Miss Sitwell's work derives from assumptions about the nature of Woman and women poets in particular. There is indeed a conception of "uniquely feminine poetry" that possesses "a feeling of personal and unanalyzable continuity with the natural world" and "womanly mysticism," [14] and such an attitude seems to be present when Mr. J. I. M. Stewart cites Edith Sitwell as "the greatest English woman poet after Emily Brontë." [15]

Related to the assumptions of a feminine and therefore "unanalyzable" mystique in Edith Sitwell's work is the belief that her poetry is without precision or shaping design, that her nature of unique talent or capricious showmanship (show*woman*ship?) knows little or no discipline. What is remarked about this poet by both her appreciators and detractors is the inexplicable, and perhaps the most memorable summation of this dimension of Edith Sitwell is from Gertrude Stein's poem in praise of Sitwell's art,

She had a way of, she had a way of not a name.[16]

This perceptive line epitomizes the response to something vaguely tonal rather than to a quality yielding to precise analysis. And it is this impression of her work which may account for the scarcity of criticism of her poetry. Critics apparently have found little to say about her.[17]

A second kind of "agreement" among the diverse critics of Edith Sitwell may be seen in the extensive silence concerning her own literary criticism. Considering that she has published many critical works of various kinds—perhaps more on poetry than any other modern poet—one might expect more acknowledgment both negative and positive, than there has been. Limitations do certainly abound in her critical work, and knowing the vigorous controversy that exists about her, one wonders why her detractors have not made more of these limitations than as opportunities for barbed quips. Similarly, those who ardently support her have articulated little of the merit which does also exist in her criticism. No explanation of this treatment really suffices. An obvious one is simply that her criticism is not taken seriously by either group, because charged as it is with personal views, it often does not conform to our contemporary insistence on the appearance of disinterest and objectivity in criticism.

One of the purposes of the examination of Edith Sitwell's criticism in the first half of this study is to demonstrate that it is not all splenetic expression of a highly eccentric taste. To those who associate only the outrageous with her and her poetry it will be a surprise to discover in her criticism a continual concern for form and a unified texture of language. An examination of her critical work reveals a duality of temperament: there is indeed the one that might be called her "way" of passionate individualism, but it is found to be joined with an abiding interest in the organic discipline of art.

Especially significant in the exposition of the disciplined esthetic that can be found in Sitwell's criticism is her frequent and unique usage of "shadow" as a term to explicate certain purposive relationships within a poem. This term is prominent in her explication of what she calls the "texture" of a poem: embodying for her the essence of interconnection, the term "shadow" clearly reveals her commitment to an organic theory of poetry, a commitment further confirmed by her many appreciative references to Coleridge.

The study of Edith Sitwell's critical writings in the opening chapters—especially the demonstration of an esthetic perception analogous to Coleridge's—is a useful introduction to the discussion of her poetry. Confronted with her dedication to integrity, a reader is encouraged to go beyond the commonplaces of criticism that her work has received and indeed question whether such an organic critic could be the formless poet that the critical clichés make her. Guided by her criticism a subsequent study of her poetry does reveal a considerable degree of order achieved not only through a rather traditional process of recurring images, but also through her unique method of repeating whole elements of poems throughout the body of her work.[18] I suggest, through analogy with Sitwell's own critical usage of the term "shadow" to indicate connection within a single poem, that these other recurring elements within her collected work are similarly unifying and may meaningfully also be called "shadows." The special emphasis she gives to the phrase "my collected work" is informed by her method of using these repeated elements to recollect a number of her poems in the realization of the total meaning of a single work.

"Meaning comes to bind the whole" is not only a line from one of her early poems: it also describes the aggregating process of the achievement of meaning in her work. Her description of a body of poetry as a "Parthenon" is by no means a capricious remark: it accords with all her architectonic interest in the order and design of all poetry, including her own.

To proceed from this analysis of a poet's organization to a study of her central symbol is a procedure especially validated by modern literary criticism. William York Tindall, defining the literary symbol as "an analogy for something unstated . . . an articulation of verbal elements that, going beyond reference and discourse, embodies and offers a complex of feeling and thought," states that "not necessarily an image, this analogical embodiment may also be a rhythm, a juxtaposition . . . a structure." [19] "We are concerned with designs," Brower writes, "as they give us access to the attitudes expressed through them." [20]

In discussing the meaning of Edith Sitwell's poetry no one has disputed the symbolist function of her work. Yet, while many symbols—Ape, Lion, Dust, Sun, Bone are prominent ones—have been adduced as evidence of her role as a symbolist, no comment has appeared on "shadow." It is, however, not only a term of Sitwell's critical vocabulary but (with its cognate "shade") even more importantly also a persistently recurring image from her earliest to her last poetry. The image of "shadow" holds a central position in the symbolist significance of her work because it embodies in its implications of interconnection all the order that her critical and poetic visions discover.

Although the demonstration of "shadow" as an important symbol—perhaps the central symbol—of her collected work is the purpose of the following study, the explication of this centrality of "shadow" necessarily includes a discussion of her symbolism of sun and darkness. Her presentation of the symbolic reconciliation inherent in "shadow" is made in part by her continuing depiction of the extremes of light and darkness as being solely in themselves "azoic" but nevertheless capable of generating life. Agreeing with Sir Thomas Browne's observation that darkness and light are both seminal states, Sitwell develops her theme of the desirability of "infinite germination" within meaningful order. The prominence of the imagery of darkness and light throughout all of her poetry in the presence of the imagery of "shadow" supports the role of "shadow" as her mediating symbol of organic order.

This evidence of the analogical symbolism of "shadow" also supports the conclusion that Edith Sitwell may indeed be a poet of metaphysical dimension for a reason other than the Crashaw-like extravagance that has been remarked in her poetry. Her employment of the image of "shadow" particularly resembles that of Donne and Marvell. (She has even described her own poetry as a "green thought in a green shade.")

The symbolic ordonnance with which she constructs her own poetic world reveals instructive affinities not only with Marvell and Donne but with the metaphysical vision in general. In this connection it is noteworthy that Edith's father, Sir George Reresby Sitwell, speaks of the metaphysical poets Herbert and Vaughan in developing his elaborate philosophy of gardens in his remarkable book, *On the Making of Gardens* (1909). Never used in any criticism of Edith—the anecdotes have it that father and daughter were never close—the evidence of his book suggests at least one realm in which the two were compatible. After a study of Sir George's book, published when his daughter was twenty-two (and still at home), it may be difficult to deny it a place with the poetry of the seventeenth century in the making of Edith's own metaphysical and symbolist poetry.

Rather than perpetuating the commonplace that Edith Sitwell is a poet of incomprehensible mystique, this study seeks to illuminate her as an artist of organic vision whose technique and symbolism reveal a central concern with order. Not solely eccentric, she works in her poetry as in her critical appreciation to construct "upon cause and reason" her analogical "empire of shade." Her vision, although personal, nonetheless is a comprehensive one which seeks in both its critical and poetic embodiment to praise the resolution of the disparate within a harmony that is most powerfully evoked in all her work by the resonating symbolism of "shadow."

JAMES D. BROPHY

Harrison, New York
June 9, 1966

Edith Sitwell
THE SYMBOLIST ORDER

1 "ELECTRIC EEL"

NO ONE has better seized the essence of Edith Sitwell's art than Yeats who remarked that "she creates . . . driven by a necessity of contrast." [1] It is this characteristic which suggests that a satisfactory critical view of her be comprehensive rather than single.

"Pride," [2] one of Dame Edith's last published prose pieces, incisively illustrates the qualifying and contrasting of elements within the body of her work. In this essay she informs us that "I have never minded being laughed at. All original artists *are* laughed at." No reader, of course, would believe Dame Edith's first statement here, for her open hostility to a host of "victims" could only be explained by her indeed having "minded" being laughed at. Dame Edith herself immediately qualifies these remarks with, "But sometimes I laugh back and that is not appreciated."

The contradiction of this sequence is meaningful. If she "sometimes" laughs back, does it not rather argue that she at least minds the laughter on those occasions? If her retaliatory laughter is not "appreciated," the tone of that laughter would seem to be hostile. If not, why would her benign laughter cause resentment? It appears that she does mind being laughed at, and we interpolate that conclusion by a comparison and reconciliation of her two contrasting statements.

The opening sentences of "Pride" present another example of her technique of qualification which is essentially ironic. "Pride has always been one of my favourite virtues" is her striking initial statement, and it is one that confirms the popular association of Dame Edith with the outrageous. Her subsequent sentence, however, is "I have never regarded it, except in certain cases, as a major sin." The resulting admission of Dame Edith that pride "in certain cases" can be "a major sin" certainly qualifies her preceding declaration, and, more importantly, qualifies any view of her (such as the prevailing one) that is based solely on that first element of her discourse. Exclusion, as Yeats saw, and as this study will demonstrate, is not the basis of Edith Sitwell's esthetic.

But even more dramatically contrasting is another juxta-position of clauses in this essay: "Pride may be my own besetting sin, but it is also my besetting virtue." The meaning of this sentence obviously must derive from the total sentence: it is clearly not that of either element nor is it the simple sum of the parts. Since the person who possesses two opposing kinds of pride is obviously not devoid of pride, the formula of the combination is not one-minus-one, but two-in-one, which situation resists fac-ile description. What is working here, and throughout Edith Sitwell's work, is the logic of comparison and con-trast where discursive elements are unstated. Like other modern poets, Sitwell imposes on the reader the burden of imaginatively reconciling in various ways her elements of diversity. Sitwell requires this process—not unlike a dialec-tic—from her beginnings as a poet and a critic.

Appropriately, considering her commitment to contrast and opposition, this present study of a reasoned order in Sitwell's esthetic confirms at the outset a contrasting dis-position: the hostility of much of her critical utterance. Her disposition to the inordinate is a qualifying part of a totality which includes the ordered. And, in a later chap-ter, I shall even suggest that the uniquely assertive repeti-tion which we shall observe in her poetry is not unrelated to the aggressive self-assertion of her critical writings.

In placing Edith Sitwell's spleen within a larger context of her work it is important to note that her first published work was verse—verse singularly devoid of any explicit attack on society. Notably, her first published piece, the short poem "Drowned Suns" (1913), reveals a tone remarkable for its revery and commonplace poetic nostalgia.

> The swans more white than those forgotten fair
> Who ruled the kingdoms that of old-time were,
> Within the sunset water deeply gaze
> As though they sought some beautiful dim face,
> The youth of all the world; or pale lost gems
> And crystal, shimmering diadems
> The moon for ever seeks in woodland streams
> To deck her cool, faint beauty. Thus in dreams
> Belov'd, I seek lost suns within your eye;
> And find but wrecks of love's gold argosies.[3]

Although we can discover here and in her other early poems some interests (darkness, sun) that pervade all her poetry, there is nothing or certainly little to suggest the biting and offensive tone of Edith Sitwell's critical remarks which will begin to appear in *Wheels. The Mother,* a collection, of five poems, published in 1915, does present, however, an interesting contrast. Three poems, including "Drowned Suns," share the same soft mood, but two other poems, "The Drunkard" and "The Mother," offer strikingly different attitudes sharply denunciatory of life lived in "a black tower" and "under the curse of God." Yet the terror that she vividly describes in these two poems is not attributed to society; the murders related in the first person are associated in some symbolic way with the personalities of the speakers. In fact, in the last lines of the title poem the mother forgives her murderer and in consummate charity takes his sin to herself.

> He did not sin. But cold blind earth
> The body was that gave him birth.
> All mine, all mine the sin; the love
> I bore him was not deep enough.

It is in the next year, 1916, with the issue of the first volume of *Wheels* that we begin to detect Edith Sitwell's critical view of society. This first issue reprints "The

Mother" and "The Drunkard," but in parts of the seven other poems of hers included in this volume we meet a vision turned outward in depreciative comment. She notes in "Gaiety," for example, that "a crumpled paper mask hides every face." Moreover, here and in several other poems we see emerge not only a Sitwell who is a critic of society, but also, even more importantly, as Yeats perceived, a poet concerned with and "driven by . . . contrast."

But it is in the supplementary issue of the first *Wheels* which the "anonymous" editor Edith Sitwell published that we first find her editorial and critical remarks (in prose). The very genesis of this issue is significant, for it is a reprint of the first volume with the addition of an appendix, "Press Notices of the First Number." Thus, the issue clearly documents the editor's interest in critical responses, and her desire to flaunt them. It is to this volume of *Wheels* and her subsequent ones which continue to print the editor's remarks that I turn for the early manifestation of Sitwell's critical temper, in particular, her "minding" of adverse criticism of her own work.

The pattern of these appendices was to print the favorable notices first, with no explicit comment. For example, the first critical section of these annual anthologies begins with a statement from the *Times Literary Supplement* that

> Edith Sitwell we have met with before, and have yielded our tribute to the pitiless strength with which she probes human suffering.

Here next, from the *Morning Post*, are the claims that "fifty years hence, the publication of 'Wheels' will be remembered as a notable event in the inner history of English literature . . ." and "the book is certain to have more influence in the future than a thousand critical brickbats or bouquets." This anonymous reviewer was perspicacious if only in sensing that "brickbats" and "bouquets" would be the kind of responses most often given to Miss Sitwell's poetry. (I might also note that he himself has presented a "bouquet.") The quotation from the *Ox-*

ford Chronicle notes that "Miss Edith Sitwell, though 'Antic Hay' shows how well she can command delight and 'The King of China's Daughter' that she can be altogether charming, presents for preference a tale like 'The Mother' of black tragedy."

Although Miss Sitwell had not listed herself as editor until the third "cycle" (as she called each issue of *Wheels*) of 1918, reticence was almost certainly not the reason, for besides the reproduction of the appreciative notices she begins her unceasing war with reviewers in the special edition of the first "cycle" by printing and annotating a response from *Poetry*. An "E.P." had written,

> Both Sacheverell and Edith Sitwell show promise; the latter using alternate ten and six syllable lines with excellent rhythmic and tonal effect but with an inexcusable carelessness as to meaning and to the fitness of expression.

Editor Sitwell, recognizing "E.P." and assuming what has become one of her characteristic roles, appended,

> Editor's Note—"We are in especial bored with male stupidity."
>
> from "The Condolence"
> by Ezra Pound.

But as we document Miss Sitwell in what has become her legendary mood, it is important to know that later she gave generous praise to Pound in her *Aspects of Modern Poetry*;[4] in her *Atlantic Book of British and American Poetry* she even calls him "one of the greatest of living poets."[5] Not only can we see extreme diversity in responses to Edith Sitwell, but we can see, as in her treatment of Pound, the extremes of Sitwell's own responses. In the next chapter I shall demonstrate how, although often rashly expressive of personal annoyance, she is also capable of a judgment more objectively based on literary criteria.

In the "Press Notices of the First Number" and "Some Opinions" sections of the first "cycle" a few depreciative remarks are printed without comment. "Its imagination is unwholesome" (*Aberdeen Journal*), "It is rather stupid to put a picture of a nursemaid wheeling a perambulator with a baby in it on the cover" (*New Statesman*), and "the foetidness of the whole clings to nostrils" (*Pall Mall Gazette*) are examples. But the editorial spirit of this compilation is an acute awareness of criticism and a sensitivity that displays the trophies not only of praise but also of rejection. The editor's comments, appended or implied by arrangement, indict and stultify the hostile responses.

The "Press Cuttings" section of the 1918 edition opens characteristically with praise from *The Nation*: "We are charmed by these ingenious and fertile able young writers," which is followed by the terse "None of them sing!" from the *Times Literary Supplement*. Here, as before, in context the initial commendation qualifies the subsequent attack. After one "Press Cuttings" a reader readily understands the intention of the contrasts, that the unfavorable notices are, to use her own phrase, "taken care of." Some depreciative reviewers, however, do (as Pound) get direct comment, for the poet and critical editor of *Wheels*—as the later Sitwell—was indeed engaged in serious, and often open, warfare with her critics.

The editor's response, in the first "cycle" to Ezra Pound was engagingly subtle in its use of his own quotation as rebuttal; in the 1918 edition of *Wheels* she replies to another unappreciative reviewer with less distinguished humor. The *Pioneer* had printed this comment.

> In "Wheels" we have discovered nothing to interest us. . . . the young authors appear to be pleased with their posturing. . . . They are apparently able to pay for the pleasure of publication, but theirs is a form of luxury which should be heavily taxed under the new scheme.

To this the Editor (still "anonymous") retorts,

> Note: Any reviewer who would like to call upon the Editor will find her happy to produce photographs of counterfoils of all the cheques sent by the contributors during the last three years.

And increasingly barbed is her reaction in the "Press Notices" section of the 1919 *Wheels*. After quoting the comments that "Edith Sitwell is a person of genius" (*Saturday Review*) and " 'Wheels' . . . has stood on the side of intelligence" (*Athenaeum*), the editor facetiously refers to the periodical *Common Cause* as "A (*Or The*) *Common Cause*" and then quotes that publication's remark.

> The title "Wheels" does suggest progress . . . Edith Sitwell remains stationary. . . . It is as though she has polished and chipped and varnished all depth and subtlety away; her obscurity is not in the least suggestive.

To this the Editor (no longer anonymous, but indeed "out in the open") appends,

> Open letter from the Editor of Wheels to Miss Jones of A (or The) Common Cause.
>
> Dear Miss Jones (if you will pardon the expression)
>
> Though the above is unsigned, I detect in it the traces, less of the cloven hoof than of a certain wooden head. I can quite understand your taking a rooted dislike to skilled technique in poetry, but may I suggest that the loss of subtlety is not always (as is the case with my poems) the result of polish. I will quote an instance to prove the reverse of your argument,—placing together Albert Samain's polished and technically perfect poem, L'Indifferent, and your translation of the same.

Editor Sitwell concludes her "letter" with

> I like you personally, Miss Jones, so I prefer to draw a veil over the rest of this painful scene, which the magic of your touch has converted from a *Fete Galante* into a family party at Lyons' Popular. Frankly, darling, what a stinker! Don't do it ever again, *please*, Miss Jones! Poetasters indeed!
>
> > Believe me, in spite of this little rift in the lute,
> >
> > Yours faithfully,
> >
> > The Editor of Wheels

But Editor Sitwell, not disposed to "draw a veil," is not yet finished with Miss Jones! The last of the "Press Cuttings," that of the 1920 edition, ends with this biting (and indeed "cutting") epitaph printed under a large cross

R. I. P. Topsy Jones

Who died defending "A Common Cause."

(Editor's Note.—Very)

"Your memory is like a well-loved book
Wherein we go continually to look."

(Editor's Note—The memorial is from the lady's published translations, and was once, alas, poor youth, Albert Samain.) [6]

Nothing is more aptly descriptive of Edith Sitwell's vituperative commentary in *Wheels* than the remark of the *Lancet* quoted in the 1920 "Press Cuttings," "We are sorry about the appendix. . . . Anything to give pain!"

Over forty years later—with an active career of similar activity in between, Edith Sitwell was still of the same disposition. As late as 1963, when she was seventy-six, she described herself as "an electric eel in a pond of catfish," [7] a remark that confirms the impression that it is she who is the aggressive party in her engagements with critics and public. Yet, without dismissing or diminishing the pain that Edith Sitwell inflicts purposefully with obvious pleasure, one is forced to observe that some of her vituperation is repayment in kind. She herself remarks in *Taken Care Of,* "I have attacked nobody unless they first attacked me." [8]

On this issue a parallel might be made with Alexander Pope, since a reading of her critical biography [9] of him suggests that in her passionate defense of Pope against his detractors (she calls them "venomous little scribblers") she sees something of her own situation. The comparison might be further confirmed by Pope's similar practice of using "press notices" for his satiric purposes in the second edition of *The Dunciad.* Although Dame Edith's provocation may have been something less than Pope's, it does appear from her ardent defense of him that she may model and justify her own outspoken career on his. His life and work do, indeed, demonstrate the possibility of combining critical spleen and formal precision, of reconciling violence and rage with order and design. It is just such contrasts that we can discern in Edith Sitwell.

One of Sitwell's best known objects of criticism is F. R. Leavis, and although he appears to have precipitated her anger by remarking in 1932 her connection with publicity, she devalues him at inordinate length—beyond any reasonable measure of "laughing back"—in her *Aspects of Modern Poetry* (1934).[10] It is relevant here to note that Mr. Leavis simply makes his remark briefly, almost in passing. Moreover, his curt statement occurs in a chapter the substance of which Miss Sitwell could hardly have quarrelled with, a chapter praising Yeats, Eliot, and her special pride, Wilfred Owen, whose poetry she introduced in the 1919 "cycle" of *Wheels,* an edition which she also dedicated to him.

As we might expect from recalling Sitwell's interment of Miss Jones, her treatment of Leavis is thoroughgoing and extensive. It is also considerably more scathing. He is associated with "dilettanti. . . . Egged on by . . . a few infant Ajaxes from the universities." And she places him "first and foremost" amongst those critics who "have a singularly debilitated, semi-puritanical dislike of beauty in poetry" (p. 20). "Dr. Leavis," she notes with elaborate caricature (p. 23),

> has a genuine, natural and cultivated gift for wincing, and this causes him . . . when probing a poem, to use phrases, graciously antiseptic, which remind one of a tenderly-ruthless, white robed young dentist.

Miss Sitwell eventually in her first chapter of *Aspects* claims to take her "leave of Dr. Leavis" but it is only to turn her satiric attack (pp. 30–31) on "the work of another critic of equal importance, Mr. Geoffrey Grigson." She hopes "that it will not offend the aunts and the other admirers of both gentlemen if I say that the only differ-

ence between them lies in Dr. Leavis' gift for wincing. Mr.
Grigson has not yet, I believe, taken up this occupation
seriously as an indoor sport." "Mr. Geoffrey Grigson," she
writes, "is not as amusing as Dr. Leavis, but there is still
considerable pleasure to be derived from contemplating
him."

As we have seen, Edith Sitwell's satiric instrument is
not usually the delicate stilletto that we might think appropriate to one of such aristocratic mien. In her spirit of
cutting open wounds, after prolonged attacks on Leavis
and Grigson, she returns to belabor both in later chapters.
As in her treatment of Pound, however, it is significant
that in *Aspects* she makes several rather generous remarks
about Mr. Leavis. And although they are too slight to
qualify substantially the intensity of her numerous attacks
(unlike her handling of Pound), the reversals confirm her
disposition to duality and contrast.

Evidence of Miss Sitwell's volatile temperament is
known to every reader, and I need adduce little more for
this introductory chapter. This aspect of her criticism
continued to her death—even posthumously in *Taken
Care of;* [11] it is, as I noted in the "Introduction," quickly
perceived and only too readily dominates her reputation.
But it is necessary, perhaps, to note further that it is Miss
Sitwell herself who has often imposed this attitude upon
us in the opening pages and chapters of books in the later
parts of which she has considerably diminished that tone.

In the "Introduction" to her *Alexander Pope,* for example, she gives little, if any, indication of her later explicative attention to esthetic aspects of Pope's poetry. Rather,
at the outset she is highly and adversely critical of her
time.

> There is a general misapprehension of the aims and of the
> necessities of poetry; and this misapprehension has arisen in
> part from the fact that many respectable persons, but very
> few poets, are encouraged to write it.

She assumes the role of antagonist immediately in her
second sentence.

The task I have given myself is a dangerous and formidable one; since whatever I say must of its very nature injure the personal susceptibilities, and make evident the lack of sensibility towards poetry, of some of our more eminent bores.

She is overtly contemptuous of many individuals.

This general blighting and withering of the poetic taste is the result of the public mind having been overshadowed by such Aberdeen-granite tombs and monuments as Matthew Arnold.

And she is also offensive.

Added to this misfortune, we are now afflicted by the shrill moronic cacklings of the Sur-Realists—laying never so much as an addled egg—and the erotic confidences of rich young ladies, suffering less from an excess of soul than from an excess of distilled spirits. All, or most of these persons, have theories or battle-cries. These theories are all very well in their way, but they do not produce poetry.

The rebuff here (and elsewhere in her work) to Matthew Arnold is informing, for no one in the mood we have been exposing seems more distant from disinterest than does Edith Sitwell. That the nature of criticism proposed by Arnold is much honored in our time may be the most apposite way of explaining the neglect and apparently low critical estimate and influence of Edith Sitwell the critic.

The opening chapter of *Aspects of Modern Poetry*, "Pastors and Masters," concludes with the remark "To such depths has the present state of criticism sunk." Regrettably the tone of hostile derision and depreciation pervades the initial section of *Aspects*, and as with her *Pope*, may label the whole work. Its aggressive extravagance is overwhelming and does not foreshadow the criticism of a different order that can be found in the remainder of the book—if one perseveres. The reader of the second chapter of *Aspects* ("Gerard Manley Hopkins") discovers the more comprehensive nature of Sitwell's criticism, the new merits of appreciative analysis which contrast with and qualify the hostile detraction that dominated the opening chapter.

The contrasting tone and statement of the second chapter immediately engages our attention.

> We have seen, in the first half of the preceding chapter, how the tactile sense, as well as energy and speed, were dying out of verse; no longer was it regarded as necessary for a poet to be in command of his material, since that material was held to be on no importance.

The disposition here to explanation is indeed markedly different from the opening chapter. For did we, in fact, there see "how the tactile sense, as well as energy and speed were dying out of verse"? As we recall the opening chapter ("Pastors and Masters") we realize that we were given little explication other than that of Dryden in the closing pages, and that is used to ridicule Wyndham Lewis. What we were given was Miss Sitwell's dunce's anthology, and what we remember is the unrestrained expression of her exacerbated displeasure. We were not shown how the concern for tactile sense, energy and speed were absent; there were no illuminating contrasts or comparisons presented; we were baldly told that Mr. Austin Dobson's lines were "wriggling horrors" (p. 22). We learned—or rather, Sitwell asserted—that the poems of O'Shaughnessy and Andrew Lang were "bloodless, nerveless escapades"; we were told of the "booming and bursting and bumping and bumptiousness of W. R. Henley" (p. 12).

In chapter one, it is Miss Sitwell's opinion that "the average uninstructed reader has, ever since the time of Shelley, Keats, Wordsworth and Coleridge, been led on one wild-goose chase after another" (p. 12). Here the critic is exposing what she does not like and quickly falls into a tone of annoyed superiority, impatience, and exaggeration. Discussing Housman and Eliot, she quotes Housman's lines,

> *And since to look at things in bloom*
> *Fifty springs are little room,*
> *About the woodland I will go*
> *And see the cherry hung with snow*

and asks, "What, for instance, do [they] add to our experience?" Her curt, and not very convincing answer is simply, "Nothing" (p. 18).

A reader might well have little desire to go beyond a first chapter which asserts about the 1890's that "any mention of the nest of a singing-bird threw the community into a frenzy" and "any simple description of a gaffer doddering in the village alehouse melted the audience to tears" (p. 19). Edith Sitwell has little that is constructive to say about the examples she presents in "Pastors and Masters," and she apparently lacks the inclination to demonstrate in critical prose a careful presentment of her judgment of what she does not like. The result is the kind of outspoken and independent assertion that we identify with the exuberance of youth, in particular, undergraduates. It is "sophomoric," although Miss Sitwell, at the publication of *Aspects of Modern Poetry* in 1934 was forty-seven! Moreover, these remarks are no different in tone from her "beginnings" in *Wheels* some fifteen years earlier when at the age of thirty she was even then long past the pardons of callow youth. Nor, in fact, is this exaggerated satire missing from her "Preface" to *Music and Ceremonies*, her last collection of poems (1963), where she writes,

> We have, at this time, a good deal too much of the Broad Church School in poetry. And the Broad Church School boys cling together, reminding me strongly of interludes in one of the later Miss Nellie Wallace's songs, in which, removing her hat, she would implore the two frondless feathers that decorate it, "For God's sake, hold together, boys!"

And continuing about the "nonsense" of verse flattened down to "lifelessness" in the past ten years, she states that "there is a good deal of yapping and snapping about 'usefulness,'" an activity she particularly associates with F. W. Bateson, but which is also an extension of her warfare with Leavis. The tone of her posthumous *Taken Care Of* is of the same nature when she is decrying "the depths to which the criticism of poetry has fallen, and the non-nutritive quality of the bun-tough whinings of certain little poetasters."

The continuity of this strain of vituperative criticism is marked by the reaction of other critics. The incisive observation of the *Lancet* (quoted above) clearly indicated that as early as 1920 her role was to *épater* the critics even more than the bourgeois. In 1953, John Malcolm Brinnin's poem (in the *New Yorker*) acknowledged her splenetic vigor at mid-century,

> She blesses, caresses, and what she dismisses
> She kills with the dart of a mot,[12]

lines which also note her contrasts of temperament. And in 1963, just a year before her death (at the age of seventy-seven), in the midst of a running battle Dame Edith was having with correspondents in the London *Times Literary Supplement,* Robert Conquest rhymed a long epic catalog of her most recent victims.

> There rose, if someone said a Sitwell
> Really didn't write a bit well
> Notional mountains of the slain,
> Around the severed head of Wain;
> —There hangs the riddled corpse of Grigson,
> Like one that Castro's turned his MiG's on;
> There, cut to pieces, lies D. Davie
> Like Ahab in the Bible (A. V.);
> Sharp as a spear you see a pen right
> Through the heart of D. J. Enright;
> That torso, red with slash and scar is
> All that's left of poor Alvarez;
> And frightful, ordered by the Dame, is
> The mayhem wrecked on Kingsley Amis.[13]

Reviewing the posthumous autobiography in 1965, Philip Toynbee remarks her "wholly distorting malice" and "dreadful follies of personal vindictiveness." [14]

The whole of Edith Sitwell's accomplishment, however, is composed of various elements, only one of which is her eccentric spleen. It is perhaps emblematic of her disposition and her work that the photograph which serves as the frontispiece of *Taken Care of* employed a mirror to portray her looking in opposite directions and that the book opens with the quotation (from Kierkegaard), "I am a Janus bifrons: I laugh with one face, I weep with the other." Besides the evisceration of authors and critics who annoy her, she reveals considerable appreciative understanding of the organic integrity of poetry. And that contrast to her olympian distemper is also important to know.

"TASTE, JUDGMENT
AND KINDLINESS"

ALTHOUGH Edith Sitwell's "electric eel" disposition is prominent and inevitably looms before us, she states in *Poetry and Criticism* (her "manifesto" according to Tindall) that "in savage criticisms . . . the true function of the critic is set aside" (p. 14). Moreover, this view is not just a passing one, for in speaking of the qualifications of the critic she quotes Ben Jonson's description of the true critic's reasoned judgment.

> The office of a true critic or censor is not to throw by a letter anywhere, or damn an innocent syllable, but lay the words together and amend them, judge sincerely of the author and his matter, which is the sign of solid and perfect learning in a man. Such was Horace, an author of much civility . . . an excellent and true judge upon cause and reason.

Even more importantly we find that the tone and method of *Poetry and Criticism* accord with these principles. She develops her case for modern poets with examples and reason. She refers to the past misunderstanding of poets such as Coleridge, Wordsworth, Keats, and Shelley by both critics and public. She refers to other critics such as Jonson, Warton, Cowley, Cocteau, and she uses the arguments and statements of Jonson, Milton, Coleridge, Wordsworth, and Shelley who have defended innovators. She compares the modern poet's position with that of "Rousseau, Picasso, Matisse, Derain, Modigliani, Stravinsky, Debussy." The use of abstraction in the past by Beddoes is adduced. And while she acknowledges (p. 22)

> the truth uttered by Blake that 'Man has no body distinct from his soul, for that called body is a portion of soul discerned by the five senses, the chief inlets of soul in this age,'

which doctrine might conceivably support a sentimental and emotional orientation of the poet—an emphasis that would be consonant with much that we commonly associate with Sitwell—we find that she does acknowledge a rational discipline and control over the senses. "The modernist poet's brain," she maintains, "is becoming a central sense, interpreting and controlling the other five senses." She indicates an elaborate theory of interrelationships when she speaks of the modern poet's senses as being "no longer little islands, speaking only their own narrow language, living their sleepy life alone. When the speech of one sense is insufficient to convey his entire meaning, he uses the language of another." Rather than impetuously intuitive, her reasoned genesis of synesthesia, indeed her whole esthetic, is recognizably philosophic and critical in the full and best senses of the words.

She quotes (p. 37), and rejects, Thomas Love Peacock's view that

> Poetry was the mental rattle that awakened the attention of intellect in the infancy of civil society; but for the maturity of mind to make a serious business of the playthings of its childhood is as absurd as for a full-grown man to rub his gums with coral and cry to be charmed to sleep by the jingle of silver bells.

And an apt characterization of *Poetry and Criticism* is the fact that the rash and hostile language is Peacock's, not hers.

Even while praising and defending innovation she speaks with restraint and respect for what is displaced (p. 16).

> Every hundred years or so it becomes necessary for a change to take place in the body of poetry, otherwise the health

and the force that should invigorate it fade. Then a fresh movement appears and produces a few great men, and once more the force and the vigour die from the results of age; the movement is carried on by weak and worthless imitators, and a change becomes necessary again. Because fresh life and vigour, and therefore change, become necessary to poetry, it does not mean that the old poets are less reverenced by the new. This change enriches the blood; it does not destroy the old, but it creates the new.

This cyclic enrichment of the poetic tradition which nonetheless "does not mean that the old poets are less reverenced by the new" sounds more than a little like Eliot's thesis of "Tradition and Individual Talent" (1917). And if she can be called derivative in this position, it is significant that she has chosen to follow in statement and in tone such a temperate critic as Eliot. Her critical relationship with Eliot in *Poetry and Criticism* is importantly qualified, however, by her consideration of Wordsworth whose battle for "the rights of ordinary speech" she defends at the same time that she states (p. 7),

> unfortunately, that liberty has by now been carried too far in some cases, and his argument that poetry is not an antithesis to prose has now been used as an excuse for the most monstrous excesses of dullness. It is therefore time that we returned to an earlier tradition in poetry.

This concept of the influence of an important poet regrettably becoming baneful, necessitating a return to an earlier tradition, brings to mind Eliot's later pronouncements on Milton (1936). It is therefore demonstrable that if Eliot's thesis is restated by Sitwell in 1926, she advances a position of Wordsworth which antedates a similar view of Eliot's.

Edith Sitwell's stated intentions in *Poetry and Criticism*, to avoid "savage criticisms," to be a Jonsonian "judge upon cause and reason" and her fulfillment of those aims in that work demonstrate that she can be an appreciative critic and is best in that role. Her *Aspects of Modern Poetry* is an even more convincing demonstration

of this observation, for in that work we see the striking
contrast of her splenetic depreciation with her more dis-
passionate explication of what does not annoy her.

We have already seen in the preceding chapter the
nature of Dame Edith's angry criticism in *Wheels, Aspects of Modern Poetry,* and *Alexander Pope.* It is an
observation that appears to justify much of the disapprobation of Edith Sitwell. As we have seen, her opening
chapter of *Aspects* (to use Bridges' remark about Hopkins'
"The Wreck of the Deutschland") is certainly another
"dragon folded at the gates to forbid entrance." [1] Yet, if
we continue in *Aspects,* we find Sitwell, as in *Poetry and
Criticism,* an appreciative critic. In the chapters that
follow "Pastors and Masters"—in "Hopkins," "Yeats,"
"W. H. Davies," "T. S. Eliot," "Sacheverell Sitwell,"
"Ezra Pound," "Notes on Innovations in Prose" (on
Joyce and Gertrude Stein), and "Envoi" (Auden, Day
Lewis, Bottrall, and Cummings)—she contributes some
illuminating criticism in her careful analyses of some of the
technical merits of these poets and writers. Even in the
concluding chapter where she has some serious reservations
about the four poets discussed, she nonetheless makes
some positively generous and appreciative remarks about
each. It is such a quality that Tindall acknowledges as her
"taste, judgment and kindliness." [2] Where she departs
from that approach and tone and turns again to satirize
(pillory is more exact) Leavis or Grigson, or where she
seeks to denounce the neglect of W. H. Davies—and
there are other instances—only then do we become op-
pressed, once again by inordinate and "savage criticisms."
Her chapter on Eliot well illustrates the nature of her
more useful and congenial criticism.

The opening of this chapter, as with the chapter on
Hopkins, is especially important, because it shows her
appreciative attitude toward her subject.

> In the year 1917, with the publication of Mr. Eliot's first
> volume, "Prufrock," began what may fairly be described as
> a new reign in poetry. The importance of the event cannot
> be exaggerated.

Significantly, perhaps because the dominant tone of approbation has been set, Miss Sitwell in continuing reveals a tone of analysis rather than of petulance towards someone like Matthew Arnold with whom she does not agree.

> The power of English poetry has been much weakened by such poets as Matthew Arnold and Dr. Bridges, who were interested equally on matter and manner, but who had not regarded these as in indivisible entity, treating them, instead, as railway lines, running side by side for a considerable time, but bearing a different set of trains bound for different junctions. In other words, applicable both to the language and metres of these poems, that language, those metres, reproduced a certain effect of relationship, and a recognizable imitation, of the theme, but did not give us the reality.

The tendency of this passage is to explain and to use "other words" than those of irascibility, although later in her essay it is important to note that in at least one instance she assumes that harsher attitude to berate a critic's "silly attempt" and "nonsensical idea" which "mutilated the rhythm" of Eliot's "Gerontion" (p. 115). But a piece of purely objective analysis would not be Sitwell's; the point of the opening chapters of this study is not that she is ever all "sweetness and light" but that she is often not derogatory or capricious. The necessity of contrast remarked by Yeats in her poetry extends even to her literary criticism. There is to be seen in her criticism much of the analytical that has been generally unremarked in her work, and the nature of this analysis is especially relevant to the developing thesis of this study: that she is essentially a poet of order and design.

In the opening paragraph of her essay on Eliot, she continues to reason her rejection of Arnold and Bridges with,

> As Coleridge said in "Biographia Literaria," "The rules of the imagination are themselves the very powers of growth and production. The words, to which they are reducible, present only the outlines and external appearance of the fruit. A deceptive counterfeit of the superficial form and

colours may be elaborated, but the marble peach feels cold
and heavy, and children only put it to their mouths."

Matthew Arnold and Dr. Bridges produced a supera-
bundance of marble peaches.

With Mr. Eliot, we are restored to a living world in
poetry.

There are at least three points of interest in the above
passage: that Sitwell quickly announces and, although she
departs from, quickly returns to the appreciation of her
subject Eliot; that her remark on Arnold and Bridges is
based on and is in the language of another critic; and most
importantly, that critic to whom she turns for support is
Coleridge.

Edith Sitwell's view of poetry, as we discover in a comprehensive assessment of her criticism, is Coleridgean. To
her the form of a poem is the totality of the statement and
feeling, and the ultimate meaning emerges from the various relationships between the elements of the poem. This
interpretation, well-known and widely accepted in our
time, is an important basis for the approaches of many
modern and "new" critics who perceive the organic nature
of a poem and treat it as a body of vital connections. It is
less known but indeed evident from what we are beginning to see of Sitwell's critical technique, from the frequency with which she quotes Coleridge and uses words
such as "organic," "vital," "architecture," and phrases like
"organic whole" that a Coleridgean esthetic is also a basis
of Edith Sitwell's work, criticism as well as poetry. There
is little doubt that the quotation from her *Notebook*, that
"the Poet accomplishes his design instinctively, but at the
same time with knowledge," [3] is a paraphrase of Coleridge's statement that composing poetry involves the psychological contraries "of passion and of will, of *sponta-
neous* impulse and of *voluntary* purpose" [4] (the italics are
Coleridge's).

The passage from Coleridge quoted above with which
Sitwell opens the chapter on Eliot is of seminal importance to her. It is, for example, obviously the source of this
statement in her chapter on Pound (p. 180).

Now [poetry] appears like the sister of horticulture—each poem growing according to the laws of its own nature, but in a line which is more often the irregular though entirely natural shape of a tree,—bearing leaves, bearing fruit.

Other quotations from Coleridge in her *Poetry and Criticism* and *A Poet's Notebook* confirm him as an important source of her concern with innate form. For example, she also includes in her *Notebook* (as she does again in *Poetry and Criticism*) this significant passage from Coleridge's *Lectures* of 1818 (p. 25).

The true . . . mistake lies in the confounding mechanical regularity with organic form. The form is mechanic, when on any given material we impress a predetermined form, not necessarily arising out of the properties of the material; as when to a mass of wet clay we give whatever shape we wish it to retain when hardened. The organic form, on the other hand, is innate; it shapes as it develops, itself from within, and the fullness of its development is one and the same with . . . its outward form.

This last quotation is especially germane to my assessment of Sitwell first as a critic and ultimately as a poet, for it presents Coleridge's recognition that "organic form," the only proper kind for art, is not to be confounded with "mechanical regularity" or, as obviously implied, with traditional rules or types of order and design. The implication of the passage, it seems, is to suggest that "organic form" is not to be found in conventional or obvious method, and that although it will be congruent with the "outward form" when found (because it is "innate"), that finding will not be easy. Certainly Coleridge implies that the discovery of "organic form" will involve some consideration beyond the superficial. If a reader or critic is to recognize "organic form" only by perceiving the "innate" with the "outward," the understanding of this organization is not likely to derive from a reading of a single or partial perspective.

But of even greater use to a study of Edith Sitwell, first as a critic and then as a poet, may be the critical method that Coleridge clearly sponsors in the above passage. If "organic form" is "innate" and "develops from within" and has no or little connection with a "mechanical" design imposed from without, then a critic under a Coleridgean aegis must limit his observation to what belongs to the creator as manifested within and by the art created. In short, the Coleridgean critic must be or strive to be something more than an impressionistic critic. He must subordinate his own nature to find the poet's.

Also, it must not be supposed from the above remarks that the poet or creator of Coleridgean disposition can be the impressionistic, that is, the uncontrollably individualistic, party either. For an organic form develops, not solely out of the poet's intuitive sensibility or primary imagination, but also from the "material," a comprehensive term that includes for Coleridge the recalcitrant realities of language and meaning. Moreover, both of these sources are confronted by what Coleridge calls the poet's "esemplastic" or shaping power. "Innate form," therefore, may come only out of a difficult process of fusion, a situation of tension, that exists between the "esemplastic" imagination and the plastic yet resisting natures of all that constitutes the poet's material. Thus, even the poet of Coleridgean dimension is by nature forced to assume a kind of humility perhaps even greater and more difficult than does the Coleridgean critic.

It can be demonstrated that Edith Sitwell, for all her attributes of imperious and eccentric "genius" (or at least for all her many manifestations of the caprice and temperament commonly associated with "genius"), in Coleridgean fashion, embodies those personal characteristics within a system of consistent design, and in Coleridge's terms possesses "shaping" as well as "genial" spirits. Moreover, even within her criticism where the submission to another artist's integrity would seem to be difficult for the poet with her own active "shaping imagination," we find her often capable of explicating a work in terms of its own informing and innate design.

She is, her own evidence of personality and "fancy"

notwithstanding, in considerable degree a critic with principles analogous to the other modern critics who also recognize Coleridge's importance. An obvious difference that exists, however, is that most of our contemporary critics deal, in their organic approaches, with meaning, and so concern themselves mostly with irony, pun, and other facets of ratiocinative statement, whereas Edith Sitwell, almost alone, emphasizes the organic form and relevance of the poem's aural aspects. In this situation, the success of Eliot's strictures on the auditory imagination announced in his first Milton essay may tend to separate Sitwell from the modern sensibility. For even though Eliot has revised his statement of Milton in 1947,[5] the aural emphasis is still of less value than the visual, in Mr. Eliot's judgment, and appears to be tolerated only as a restorative until modern poetry loses some of its excessive likeness to prose. Sitwell's emphasis on the aural serves to exaggerate her individuality and obscure the demonstrable fact that she too in part derives from Coleridge.

In this concern with the aural nature of poetry she indicates her own isolation in recognizing that

> there is a general lack of interest in the fabric of poetry. Many people have no feeling for or knowledge of that quality which my friend Mr. Robert Graves calls "texture."

The "texture," which she defines in Graves' words, covers

> the relations of a poem's vowels and consonants, other than rhymes, considered as mere sound, and supplementing the rhythm and images. It will . . . include the variation of internal vowel sounds to give an effect of richness; the use, perhaps, of liquid consonants and labials and open vowels to give smoothness, of aspirates and dentals to give strength; the careful use of sibilants which are to texture what salt is to food.[6]

It is her concern for this "texture" that characterizes her analysis in *Aspects of Modern Poetry* of the first verse of that "great poem, 'The Wreck of the Deutschland.' "

> *Thou mastering me*
> *God! giver of breath and bread;*

World's strand, sway of the sea;
Lord of living and dead;
Thou has bound bones and veins in me,
    fastened me flesh,
And after it almost unmade, what with dread,
Thy doing: and dost thou touch me afresh?
Over again I feel thy finger and find thee.

Sitwell tells us that

In the slow and majestic first line, the long and strongly-swelling vowels, and the alliterative M's, produce the sensation of an immense wave gathering itself up, rising slowly, ever increasing in its huge power, till we come to the pause that follows the long vowel of "me." Then the wave falls, only to rush forward again.

After this majestic line comes the heaving line
    "God! giver of breath and bread,"
ending with the ship poised on the top of the wave. This last effect is caused by the assonances of "breath and bread." The sound of "breath" is slightly longer, has slightly more of a swell beneath the surface than "bread," because of the "th."

In her line-by-line description (pp. 59–60) we learn that "this pause on the top of the wave is followed by the gigantic straining forward of the waves in the line 'World's strand, sway of the sea' " which is

an effect that has been produced by the strong alliterative S's, reinforced by the internal R's of "World's strand," followed by the internal W of "sway." This line, after the huge tossing up and down from the dulled A of "strand" to the higher dissonantal A of "sway," ends by sweeping forward still further with the long vowel-sound of "sea," a sound that is more peaceful than that of "strand" and "sway" because of the absence of consonants.

Sitwell's analysis of the "texture" or "fabric of poetry" is not exclusively concerned with internal sounds, as is the above passage and as her definition may imply. We note, for example, that she discusses in *Aspects* the texture of only the end-rhymes of Yeats' "Crazy Jane on God." "In this poem," she writes, "the impression of those torn rags of womanhood"

> *a house*
> *That from childhood stood*
> *Uninhabited, ruinous,*
> *Suddenly lit up*

is conveyed by the tuneless half-rhymes that appear from time to time: "would-God" (a plunge into immeasurable depths, this) in the first verse; "sky-neigh," "tread-God," "was-pass" in the second verse; "house-ruinous" (the extra syllable in the second word gives a feeling of huddled misery), "stood-God," "up-top" in the third; "lover-over," "road-God," "moan-on" in the fourth.

There may indeed be some question about what, in the statement below, Sitwell terms the "psychological significance" of this explication, but there can be no question that this critic also implicates us closely with the details of the text. Following her we can neglect no aural attribute (pp. 88–89).

It is a memorable fact that the only pure rhymes are in the first verse (where there is still the "would-God" half-rhyme on which I have commented already) and this has much psychological significance. In the second verse, there is a mixture of rising, falling, and stretching half-rhymes or dissonances; in the third all are falling; in the last verse, the half-rhymes alternately fall and stretch wildly into infinity. This is one of the deeply significant technical interests of this great poem.

We note that this criticism is appreciative exposition, in marked contrast to her depreciative exasperation. Moreover, the considerable subjective element of this interpretation is "upon cause and reason," constructed upon textual realities of the poem.

Sitwell writes that "Words for Music," from which "Crazy Jane on God" is taken, are "undoubtedly the greatest lyrics of the last hundred years, because of their intense fusion of spirit and matter." Yet, in regard to the organization of what she calls the "texture" of a poem she is more engaged, in *Aspects of Modern Poetry*, with T. S. Eliot, although Eliot ironically has more than any critic depreciated the auditory that is Sitwell's main concern. In praising "Prufrock" she even speaks again with an attitude comparable to Eliot's own in "Tradition and the Individual Talent" (and to hers in *Poetry and Criticism*) in noting that *The Love Song of J. Alfred Prufrock and Other Poems* were a "shock to persons clamoring for a cul-de-sac in the guise of tradition," but that "to informed traditionalists they should have presented no difficulty, since they are a logical development" of the past. She finds, as Eliot himself, that a qualified originality, one that grows within a tradition and is not absolutely original, is best. And in this, one remarks again a modification of her role as an extravagant individualist.

While retaining her dedication to growth and relationship which embraces tradition, she also finds Eliot's poetry important, because she also finds it "vital" with a "muscular system of the verses" that "arises from that of the poet, and is inherent in the needs of the poems." Continually revealing this Coleridgean interest in the organic totality of a work of art she praises the "architecture" of Eliot's poetry, and states that its "rhythms flow, change, shift their forms, melt into other rhythms according to the needs of the subject." "The architecture of Mr. Eliot's poems," she writes, "must be . . . described in these words of Emerson" (p. 102),

> It is not metres, but a metre-making argument, that makes a poem—a thought so passionate and alive that, like the spirit of a plant or an animal, it has an architecture of its own, and adorns nature with a new thing.

With this organic commitment to unity she analyzes the opening lines of "Prufrock" for the relevance between texture and meaning (p. 103).

> The fact that the first heavily accented word in the first line is the word "go" gives a necessary touch of determination to this poem of indecision. The line "When the evening is spread out against the sky"—though it is actually

of exactly the same length as the next line—both have a half-muted fraction of a syllable beyond their norm: ("evening," "table") bringing to mind the dumb softness of this half-light—appears to be slightly longer, more wearied, because of the mound of "evening" (a mound caused by the extra half-syllable), whereas "table" though it begins with a flat stretch of sound, ends with the muted fraction of a syllable, falling away to nothingness.

Here, the critic appears to be doing what Eliot has defined as the function of the intelligent and perfect critic; that is, "swiftly operating the analysis of sensation to the point of principle and definition." [7] This is similar to the kind of analysis we find the exacting textual critic Reuben Brower making in his discussion of the voice of Mary in Frost's "Death of the Hired Man."

Her sentence rhythm has its breaks of another sort—the hesitant pauses of someone reaching for the right word, qualifying, softening harsh statements of fact. The syntax is less neat and efficient, the sentences broken by asides and slightly repetitious—deft notations of feminine incoherence.[8]

A critic reviewing Brower's work finds that "knowledge and feeling are united here, typically, in an act of critical intelligence." [9] Edith Sitwell, in a final analysis, is not the reasoned and tactful critic which we find Brower to be, but it is pertinent here to note that at times there is more than a slight resemblance between Sitwell's criticism and the dominant method of our era. It is difficult, if not impossible, to distinguish from a number of contemporary critics the author of a statement like this (about the opening of "Prufrock"),

Here then, we have not only the beginning of Mr. Eliot's amazing genius for handling his material, but also the beginning of that power of creating a universe by making all time as one, by fusing all experience into one, after a long process of deliberate disintegration.[10]

Edith Sitwell, here and throughout her work, reveals her basis of fidelity to the integral and autonomous nature of a poem, a view which she shares with many contemporary critics. Moreover, her rejection of a moral basis for criticism—a rejection evident in her work and explicitly stated in *Poetry and Criticism* (p. 37)

> When we are told that a poem cannot be a great poem unless it be built on a lofty moral theme, it is obvious that this belief is based on a total misapprehension of the nature of poetry.

—further strengthens her analogy to the textual critics.

Brower writes in his *Fields of Light* that critics agree that there are important functions of sound in poetry but "beyond general agreement of this sort chaos begins, especially when critics try to demonstrate more particular relations between sound and sense, or between what is heard and design" (p. 58). This statement well expresses the hesitancy of textual critics to indulge in the impressionism that to them inheres in the annotation of the auditory. Nonetheless, Brower himself proceeds, as he did in the comment on Frost's poem above, to analyze George Herbert's "The Windows" in a manner that tries to demonstrate the very kind of "particular relationship between sound and sense" that we have just seen Brower apprehensive of. In his analysis of the stanza,

> *Doctrine and life, colours and light, is one*
> *When they combine and mingle, bring*
> *A strong regard and aw: but speech alone*
> *Doth vanish like a flaming thing,*
> *And in the eare, not conscience ring*

he writes (p. 61),

> In the next line, "bring" (which gets a somewhat similar emphasis because of position) belongs to an odd chain of rhymes and assonances: "mingle . . . bring . . . flaming thing . . . ring." We must—with considerable tact— slightly lengthen each of the -ing-ring syllables, "entuning it through the nose." (Herbert would be expert at this we suppose.) By this chain of recurrent sounds we make up a kind of "poetic morpheme": we feel the sense of "ring" in words of very different meaning. So we are kept close to the

physical fact, the heard voice of the holy Preacher. When
we hear "ring" in the word which is also an image of light
we experience, in little, the fusion of light and sound which
is central in the poem. The force with which we come
down on the final "ring,"

> *And in the eare, not conscience ring*

suggests by analogy the eloquence that resounds in the
inner life.

This is much like Edith Sitwell's analysis of what she calls
"texture," and the practice of this kind of criticism by
Brower who is indeed apprized of its pitfalls may indicate
the need there is in textual criticism to experience in the
word "the fusion of light and sound which is central in
the poem."

The example of a critic like Brower analyzing "the
figure of sound" in what may be unavoidably impressionistic terms can be adduced in the demonstration that Edith
Sitwell's impressionism, employed as it is to elucidate
structure, does not negate the Coleridgean basis of her
belief that "the texture and the subject form one miracu-
lous whole." There is, of course, a difference between
Brower and Sitwell, and it lies in Brower's greater recognition of the burden on the textual analyst. There is in his
work—as he mentions above there must be—"considerable
tact" in his presentation. This explicative "tact" is frequently missing from Dame Edith's critical writing even
where her splenetic temper is under control.

A reader continually wishes that Edith Sitwell realized
how untrained her fellow critics and readers are in her
kind of analysis. Assuredly, in the following passage from
Aspects on the rhythmic subtleties of Eliot's "Rhapsody
on a Windy Night," she is instructive to many besides the
"listener unused to, or only half-educated as to, verse,"
whom she claims to address (p. 104).

I have known an unskilled listener (by which I mean a
listener unused to, or only half-educated as to, verse,)
misled on hearing this poem for the first time, misled by
the *balance*, in spite of the constant change from the sober

walking movement of some of the lines, into the running movement of other lines, now short, now long—into believing that these are not only sharply and closely rhymed *externally*, but from time to time, *internally* also.

Undoubtedly she directs many skilled readers (skilled, that is, in other approaches to a poem) to discover something more "of the extreme control in which the poem is held." But what Sitwell appears not to realize sufficiently is that even skilled readers need to be taught the perception of a "walking movement" or a "running movement."

She does, however, seem to know something of the necessity for detailed and explicative criticism in this kind of exposition. For one thing, the considerable detail that she does present indicates that she is acquainted with the need, and in *Aspects of Modern Poetry* (p. 142) she has quoted and agreed with Allen Tate's observation that

> When we read poetry we bring to it the pseudo-scientific habit of mind; we are used to connecting things up in vague disconnected processes in terms that are abstract and thin, and so our sensous enjoyment is confined to the immediate field of sensation.

She who has supported this statement and who has gone on to add that "it is exactly this belief that poetry should be only a pseudo-philosophy expounding pseudo-scientific ideas, that has prevented . . . an intense and wide sensuous enjoyment" must presumably see some necessity for carefully teaching an aural enjoyment and analysis of poetry. The question arises, of course, whether Sitwell—or anyone—can effectively demonstrate the aural distinction between a "sober walking movement" and "the running movement of other lines." Regrettably, Miss Sitwell frequently does not attempt the extended explication which we would welcome.

But to make these demands on this critic is perhaps only to illustrate the difficult burden placed on any critic who would attempt what Sitwell does. We can well understand why a critic like Brower who likes to "discuss what we can discuss" [11] avoids interpretation of the aural as much as he does. Yet, regardless of how satisfactory or useful some of Sitwell's analysis is, there is no doubt about her continuous dedication to the fundamental Coleridgean doctrine of organic design. She concludes her analysis of "Rhapsody on a Windy Night" in *Aspects* (p. 105) remarking that

> occasional rhymes, placed purposely at certain points in the poem, seem to gather together, within the region of one space and time, all these old memories of things seen and experienced, things which would otherwise lie scattered throughout space and throughout time. These rhymes, gathering together and enclosing these scattered things within our universe, occur by the laws of nature and not by a superimposed law.

When she undertakes work on this basis, as she often does,—when she is a critic aware of an ordered integrity—she is, indeed, in addition to an "electric eel" also a Coleridgean critic.

Her attention to the "scattered things" that a poet must gather together leads her often to demonstrate the connections between different sections of a poem. For example, in *The Waste Land* she notes that "the deep and holy passion" of the passage about the hyacinth girl,

> *You gave me hyacinths first a year ago*
> . . . .
> *Your arms full, and your hair wet, I could not*
>   *Speak . . .*

will soon be changed to this terrible echo (in "A Game of Chess").

> *My nerves are bad to-night. Yes, bad, stay with me.*
> *Speak to me. Why do you never speak. Speak.*

"In the rest of the passage," Miss Sitwell writes, "the weft left over from the 'empty shuttles of the wind' is mainly composed of two threads, 'do' and 'nothing,' and an echo of this floats towards us, drifting still more aimlessly, with all the life gone out of the wind, in 'The Fire Sermon.'"

On Margate Sands.
I can connect
Nothing with nothing.

For Eliot, as for Sitwell, the mark of despair and dissolution is disconnection, and her primary interest in Eliot as explicated in *Aspects of Modern Poetry* (p. 130) has been to reveal "his supreme genius for organizing a poem."

Edith Sitwell's commitment to the informing unity and organization of a poem is nowhere better seen than in her criticism of "The Rape of the Lock" (in her *Alexander Pope*). Since she tells us in *Taken Care Of* that she had memorized the poem before she was thirteen, it is not surprising that in her *Pope* she makes a "close" reading of the work and, in fact, seeks to analyze the very weave of its texture. Her question, "This thin and glittering texture, how did it ever come into being?" (p. 221) is unlike Cleanth Brooks' inquiry into the logical meaning of the poem.[12] But her answer is also from the poem itself, "The whole poem might have been woven by the air-thin golden fingers of Pope's sylphs. . . . The lines differ in no wise from the wings of the sylphs, as they float above the barge,"

> *Some in the sun their insect-wings unfold,*
> *Waft on the breeze, or sink in clouds of gold;*
> *Transparent forms, too fine for mortal sight,*
> *Their fluid bodies half-dissolved in light.*
> *Loose to the wind their airy garments flew,*
> *Thin glittering textures of the filmy dew,*
> *Dipped in the richest tincture of the skies,*
> *Where light disports in ever-mingling dyes;*
> *While ev'ry beam new transient colours flings,*
> *Colours that change whene'er they wave their wings.*

Hers is also a textual criticism. If it may seem fanciful (using Coleridge's meaning) to say that "the whole poem might have been woven by the air-thin fingers of Pope's sylphs," we have to concede that at least the "fancy" grows from and seems shaped by Pope's own "material." We are reminded by Brooks himself, moreover, that "we miss the whole point if we dismiss the sylphs as merely 'supernatural machinery,' " for the "sylphs . . . symbolize the polite conventions which govern the conduct of maidens." [13] If the poem's meaning is integrally related to the sylphs, as Brooks claims it is, then Sitwell's discussion of the poem's sound in those same terms is also valid, assuming, of course, that the poet's creative imagination has fused sound and meaning into an organic whole as Coleridge would expect in a successful poem. Besides, if we wish to be true to Pope's own creative logic, his famous dictum in *An Essay on Criticism*, "The sound must seem an Echo to the sense," well indicates Pope's concern in this matter.

Continuing to explicate the nature of "This thin and glittering texture" Sitwell notes the "control of texture . . . with the light and lovely liquids of the earlier lines, and the richer colour of the last two couplets" (p. 221). Her interest in the integrity of the poem leads her to "compare the lines quoted above, with the description of the card-party, in the Third Canto, with the velvety softness, and depth and shade—like the shadow cast by a great tree on some hot afternoon,"

> And parti-coloured troops, a shining train,
> Draw forth to combat on the velvet plain.
> The skilful nymph reviews her force with care.
> Let spades be trumps: she said, and trumps they were.
> Now move to war her sable matadores,
> In show like leaders of the swarthy Moors.
> Spadillo first, unconquerable lord!
> Let off two captive trumps, and swept the board.

She also compares this passage "with the early morning whiteness of the First Canto" to show how the "thin, glittering texture" is not monotonous but skillfully various. But again, we might ask, is not her description of the Third Canto as possessing "velvet softness, and depth and shade—like the shadow cast by a great tree on some hot afternoon" and her characterization of the First Canto as "morning whiteness" not an intrusion of her own impressions into Pope's poem? The answer suggests that there is less imposition of Edith Sitwell's personal feeling than is first apparent.

The difficulty here as throughout her criticism is that she expects us to come to close terms with aural intricacies of the text in a way that few readers are accustomed or prepared to do. In this particular case, one can defend some of what appears to be sheer personal association by pointing out that Sitwell's "velvety softness" derives from Pope's "velvety plain" where the card-game battle is being waged. More subtly the "depth and shade" and "shadow" are justified by the poem's "sable matadores" and "swarthy Moors," the blackness of Spades and Clubs and (lest we forget) the very name of the game which is central to the Canto—*Ombre*.

Sitwell may speak of "some hot afternoon" because Pope's scene takes place when

> *declining from the noon of day*
> *The sun obliquely shoots his burning ray.*

And as for the First Canto's "morning whiteness," the time of that scene is morning and the imagery, to use Pope's adjectives, is "white," "glittering," "silver," and "gilded." Upon consideration Sitwell indeed appears to have a critic's necessary intimacy with the text, and frequently makes explicit use of its details: "Pope used female rhymes twice, if 'flowers' may be held to be a female ending." Her textual scrutiny can be illustrated by her comment on the lines,

> *The meeting points the sacred hair dissever*
> *From the fair head, for ever, and for ever!*

of which she says, "It is interesting to notice the extra emphasis like a cry, obtained by the use of an internal rhyme." Undoubtedly, to many readers of her exposition the reference to "cry" is disconcertingly arbitrary. But Sitwell does not print as part of her presentation the subsequent lines from the "Rape."

> *Then flashed the living lightning from her eyes*
> *And screams of horror rend the affrighted skies*

which suggest that the preceding lines might well prepare for and anticipate the "screams of horror" with a "cry." That the insistence, through the internal rhyme of "hair"-"fair," of the previous lines is on the cause of the forthcoming "screams" also tends to unite the two elements. The choice of "cry" to label a call of attention (which is what rhyme is) under these textual circumstances is then quite reasonable.

A final example of her treatment of Pope may suffice to show the unique character of Sitwell's criticism. She writes in her *Pope* (p. 223) that

> The clearest proof of the extraordinary subtlety of Pope's use of texture is that we actually notice the little cool shadows of that extra fraction of a syllable, so slight that it is hardly audible, contained in the rhythms of this couplet:

> *A brighter wash; to curl their waving hairs,*
> *Assist their blushes, and inspire their airs.*

Again, we feel, she can be accused of understatement in that "the extra fraction of a syllable" is probably noticed by few, if anyone, besides Miss Sitwell. It certainly does not constitute the "clearest proof," especially as she presents her observations. She continues to tell us (rather than explain) that

> The words "airs," "hairs" have a little wavering sound, like the slight breath of a summer air among young leaves. And this is not only the result of association. We find this tiny freshening sound several times in the poem.

Here the critic attempts to sharpen our aural perception of the poem and enable us to accept her description of the diphthong phenomena as "wavering," which if true would indeed be an excellent example of Pope's achieving a fusion of sound and sense. But lacking the "tact" of a critic like Brower and the disposition to annotate explication that generally typifies the "new" critics she does not fully succeed in convincing her reader. When she writes "we find this tiny freshening sound several times in the poem," we should like to have from her (as we do in Brooks' annotation of the poem) a detailed description of the reoccurrences. And why does she protest, "And this is not only the result of association"? If we could see what the association could be, her point would be stronger. The point is that the immediately preceding lines—again not quoted by the critic—refer to "gale," "exhale," and "vernal flowers."

> *Our humbler province is to tend the fair,*
> *Not a less pleasing, though less glorious care;*
> *To save a powder from too rude a gale,*
> *Nor let the imprisoned essences exhale;*
> *To draw fresh colours from the vernal flowers.*

Although the critic herself here wishes to discount "association," it is important to know that it is Pope's imagery that resonates within Sitwell's critical consciousness, and that to some degree Edith Sitwell is giving us Pope's organic synthesis.

Yet, granting that the terms of this critic are related to the poet's and that she continually presumes the kind of organic and technical integrity that the poet may well have intended, it is not always possible to assent with certainty to her analysis. Perhaps this is so because of the ellipsis that intervenes between the textual genesis of her terms and her use of them. We often feel Sitwell's logic more insistently than we are sure of Pope's, but this may only be due to her reluctance to explain certain important steps of her analysis. These lacunae are puzzling, but they are typical of her prose style.

One explanation of both her detailed commentaries and her cryptic omissions may simply be that she wrongly assumes the reader knows the text as well as she.[14] But a more satisfying reason may use Yeats' perception that she is "driven by a necessity of contrast." The need to assert herself may be appeased by the impressionistic appearance of her critical approach at the same time that her critical conscience would be served by the actual but veiled and subtle association of her impressions with the text under discussion. Whatever the reason, it is easy to understand how these impressionistic elements joined with her "electric eel" disposition have established Edith Sitwell as sibylline and eccentric.

Moreover, Dame Edith herself has often contributed to this reputation by explicitly stating her distance from the ordered and rational. For example, in the preface to her collection *The Pleasures of Poetry* she announces, "I have no settled plan in making this collection of poems; they are arranged by no rule." [15] Under this light a reader certainly has reason to see no "cause and reason" in her work. Yet, she continues—with the kind of contrast that can be seen throughout her work, and in particular in her essay on pride—to say

> my only excuse for the book is that, to enliven a tiresome illness of three month's duration, I longed to gather together some poems that I loved; and so I have picked them, with delight, as one picks wild flowers, and have made them into a country bunch.

Furthermore, she has "seized, for the most part, those poems which do not, as a rule, appear in anthologies." Thus, one finally discovers that she does have a "settled plan" and that she does shape variety into unity: the unity of a "country bunch" of poems with the shared characteristic of being "loved" by her and not generally anthologized. In the final analysis she has, indeed, "made" something. The subtitle of *The Pleasures of Poetry*, "A Critical Anthology," is therefore justified. Again the careful reader finds in Edith Sitwell's work not only the exhibition of idiosyncrasy and an impressionism that appears to spring from some inner (and perhaps inexplicable) drive, but also a contrasting recognition of form and critical direction.

The criticism of Edith Sitwell examined in this chapter reveals that essentially a Coleridgean she shares with Coleridge and those who derive from him, including "new" critics, a basic concern with the informing organization of a poem. Through a study of her critical term "shadow" the following chapter will make the even more important demonstration of the intellective order which she critically observes in her own poetry.

3 "SHADOW"
AND INTERNAL ORDER

IN EDITH SITWELL'S exegesis of the organization of a poem
no term or concept—with the possible exception of "texture"—is more significant than "shadow." Although she
also employs the term "echo" to describe a repetitive
aspect of a poem's structure, and although in some instances she appears to use "echo" in a way similar to her
use of "shadow," it is evident in a close study of her
criticism that she does assign different meanings and functions to these two terms.

A remark from her comparison of her brother Sacheverell's poetry with "Lycidas" (in *Aspects of Modern Poetry*)
illustrates one important basis of her differentiation: "A
dark and mournful air moves through all these strange
lines, so full of long shadows, so full of lengthening echoes
dying away into a silence that is like music" (p. 153).
These phrases denoting the "shadows" and "echoes" are
not synonymous or appositive: consistent with what we
shall find her usage elsewhere we realize that "shadows"
endure and "echoes" die away. Both activities may, of
course, have a place in the organic form of a poem, but it
is the term connoting permanence, the term which describes the enduring bond between elements, that better
serves the vision of unity in multiplicity which underlies
her esthetic.

"Shadow" is a critical concept that grants body and
endurance to the sustaining source; "echo" implies that
the origin has passed in time and that only a fleeting or

"dying" likeness of it remains. Moreover, "shadow" suggests difference or contrast, the complexity of reality, whereas "echo" is more closely limited to the reproduction of the similar. In *Aspects of Modern Poetry* (p. 105) it is with the richer meaning of "shadow," therefore, that Edith Sitwell describes

> Mr. Eliot's power of attaining to an extraordinary compression and expressiveness, of conveying all the complexities of a character by means of fusing two widely opposed points of time—each throwing strong shadows of their widely different significances.

It is this meaning that particularly informs her description of the "poetry which followed that of Swinburne, the two Rossettis and Tennyson" as being "flat and thin, or shallow and shadowless" (p. 73).

Diversity, multiplicity, polarity—the contrast missing from much Victorian poetry and for which Yeats remarked her "necessity"—are the abiding concern of Edith Sitwell's work. It is a note sounded from her first critical essay, her introduction to her *Children's Tales From the Russian Ballet* (1920), where she denounces the persistent single vision of "petits bonheurs" that often caused the "English music hall stage" to present a "distorting mirror" of "mechanical life." "Before the arrival of the first company of the Russian Ballet in England," she writes, "the average person had never dreamt that movement could convey a philosophy of life as complete and rounded as any world could be." In the art of the Russian Ballet she found realized "the clearer philosophy . . . not of a mood alone, but often of life itself . . . now the intense vitality of the heart of life, now the rigidity of death." Praising the "terrible gaity" of Laforgue, she reveals in this essay her disposition to the ironic bond of opposition that for her constitutes the "complete and rounded" life. It is exactly such an ironic integrity embodied in the vitality of a poem that is served by the function of "shadow."

Understandably, Sitwell finds a kind of Laforguian vision in Eliot, who she states in *Aspects* (p. 105) "has been able to draw together figures, symbols, and events, which otherwise lie scattered throughout Time and Space. To Sitwell, "the whole scope" of *The Waste Land* "is concentrated, made small for our inspection in these lines.

> *Here, said she*
> *Is your card, the drowned Phoenician Sailor,*
> *(Those are pearls that were his eyes. Look!)*
> *Here is Belladonna, the Lady of the Rocks,*
> *The lady of situations.*
> *Here is the man with three staves, and here the Wheel,*
> *And here is the one-eyed merchant, and this card,*
> *Which is blank, is something he carries on his back,*
> *Which I am forbidden to see. I do not find*
> *The Hanged Man. Fear death by water.*
> *I see crowds of people, walking round in a ring.*

Significantly, these "scattered" aspects, for Sitwell, are bound up with "shadows." "The way in which caesuras are cast throughout the passage," she writes, "gives the impression that they are lengthening shadows; and perhaps for this reason, the clairvoyante's voice seems to be that of a sleepwalker, wandering amongst the shadows, rather than that of a sibyl amidst the desert lights of day" (p. 127).

Typically, as discussed in the previous chapter, this comment of Sitwell's is difficult to understand, and without expansion and annotation by the reader it may be of limited use in explaining the passage. For example, to understand fully the use of "shadow" here one should know what Sitwell does not give us: Eliot's immediately preceding lines on "shadow."

> *Only*
> *There is shadow under this red rock,*
> *(Come in under the shadow of this red rock),*
> *And I will show you something different from either*
> *Your shadow at morning striding behind you*
> *Or your shadow at evening rising to meet you.*

Eliot's use of "shadow" as an image and symbol of the inter-relationships of reality reinforces Sitwell's statement.

A reader knowing neither Sitwell's own special use of "shadow" nor the role of "shadow" in Eliot's context might indeed find Sitwell's a riddling commentary. Even with that information one might still wish to know more about how the "caesuras are cast" to give the "impression of lengthening shadows." Yet, whatever information is withheld, it is certainly possible and important to know in the understanding of Sitwell's work that "shadows" are the agents of whatever unity Sitwell sees in this passage. The heterogeneous elements of Madame Sosostris' world (and her "bad cold" suggests that it is our world too) touch only through the function of "shadows." And even before the further explicative work of this chapter it is possible to detect the special implications of connective order with which Edith Sitwell endows the term.

In ascertaining the use and importance of "shadow" to Sitwell further definition may be seen in her discussion in *Aspects* (p. 148) of Sacheverell Sitwell's "Dr. Donne and Gargantua." This is a poem which, partly in Sacheverell's words, she describes as of "the two shadow worlds, the real and metaphysical" which "march side by side in their endless and hopeless battle." Using her conception of "shadow," Edith gives a technical description of the effect caused by the assonances ending the lines,

> *Doomed to a clown's death, laughing into old age,*
> *Never pricked by Brutus in the statue's shade.*

She writes that

in the change from the sound of "age"—a sound which has body, but which seems crumbling and shrinking into dust (perhaps because of the faint shrinking shadow thrown by the "ge" coming after the long A), in the change from this to the slightly longer and flatter sound of "shade," with the menacing, shuddering beginning (actually "shade" is a kind of reversed shadow of "age," a shadow falling backwards, since the "sh" is a sort of flatter echo of the "ge"), in this change, preceded by the far shorter A of "statue," less long, less real, than the lengthening shadow that is thrown by it, we have the change from the crumbling physical world to that world of untouchable reality which lies about us.

In this explication of a rigorously close reading we learn that through the presence of a "shadow" we have the presence of one element felt (heard and seen) in another. "Age" denoting Gargantua's world of time "seems crumbling," but it is the connection to "shade," Donne's world of spirit, that is of more importance. "Age" is perceived in "shade" through the function of what Edith Sitwell calls "shadow," and in this phenomenon the lines technically reinforce the poem's sense of Dr. Donne and Gargantua "marching side by side," together yet apart—in a sense the contrast and reverse of each other.

This passage also well demonstrates why "shadow" rather than "echo" is the more appropriate term for Sitwell's intricate relationships of connection. An "echo" of "age" would logically have to die out, which demise would leave the world of "shade" eventually untouched by "age." Yet that is not what the poem presents: the two symbolic figures march side by side in "unending" battle. The duality is to persist. The physical world is to be always crumbling, and the spiritual "untouchable reality" is to always lie about us. We can will that one of these worlds be triumphant or ascendant over the other, but in the poem "age" is caught in a suspended change to "shade"; in the poem, as in life, there are complexity and contrast and tension rather than singularity. Such a full and rounded reality might indeed incorporate "shadow." It was, we remember, the thin and shallow world of Victorian poetry that Sitwell characterized as "shadowless."

In addition, if one is to utilize the meaning of inversion—as here in her discussion of the change from "age" to "shade"—it is more meaningful to conceive, as she does, of a "reversed shadow" than a reversed echo. A shadow can be reversed with more conceivable meaning than can an echo, which when inverted tends to nonsense. E. M. Forster's account in A *Passage to India* of the incident in the Marabar Caves may be an especially convincing illustration of the sense of chaos that accompanies the distortion of an echo. In her criticism of poetry Edith Sitwell has use for a term which conveys the maximum intelligence of the uniquely intricate order which she finds inherent in the texture of a successful poem.

Although John Lehmann in his pamphlet[1] on Edith Sitwell treats her criticism with only "a few words," mentioning neither *Poetry and Criticism* nor *Aspects of Modern Poetry,* he does appositely remark that her *Alexander Pope* "tells one almost as much about the author as about Pope" (p. 33). And although he (as most critics) is primarily concerned with her "sibylline mode," "incomparable manner," "deep intuitive sympathy" and "her battle against the state of poetry," he also remarks that a quality she shares with Pope is "the tremendous force of intellect which he packs into his work" (p. 32).

Lehmann's remark is perceptive. As we saw in the previous chapter there may be some question as to whether the effects that Sitwell describes are Pope's or hers, and beyond that consideration, if we can reconstruct what she experiences. But there is no doubt about her own intellectual commitment to the order and design which she observes in Pope's text. An important use of her criticism may well be suggest that she is the kind of a poet which she sees others to be. This hypothesis is further strengthened by the nature of the analysis she has made of her own poetry: like all of her appreciative studies of other poets it stresses organization of a unique kind and degree.

The poet's explication of her own poetry is no less difficult than her close analysis of other poets which we observed in the preceding chapter. The poet, moreover, makes no apology for the highly organized poem that elicits and demands such a response. She writes in "Some Notes on My Poetry" that

> The poems in *Façade* are abstract poems—that is, they are patterns in sound. They are too, in many cases, virtuoso exercises in technique of an extreme difficulty, in the same sense as that in which certain studies by Liszt are studies in transcendental technique in music.[2]

One can well understand, therefore, why she says "we must not complain . . . if the patterns in the humble works of Man are not perceived immediately by the unobservant." Yet one must not be misled by this statement to believe that Miss Sitwell has become charitable toward or even tolerant of these "unobservant." In typically contrasting fashion she continues her remarks, adding, "Therefore, to rebukes and protests, I returned the answer 'God comfort thy capacity,' and went on my way" (p. xvi).

The "way" of Edith Sitwell is indeed involute. But while there is truth in Lehmann's observation that "there will always be more in her poetry than can be elucidated in mere prose analysis," such a position, as I shall continue to stress, too much emphasizes the ineffable qualities of her sibylline characteristics. Her poetry under her own study becomes, rather than intuitive and elusive, an intricate pattern of order and direction that yields to examination. Sitwell's analysis of her own work suggests that discursive explication of her poetry may indeed be possible.

One of her most instructive analyses is of her poem "Said King Pompey" (from *Façade*, 1922).

> Said King Pompey, the emperor's ape,
> Shuddering black in his temporal cape
> Of dust, "The dust is everything—
> The heart to love and the voice to sing,
> Indianapolis,
> And the Acropolis,
> Also the hairy sky that we
> Take for a coverlet comfortably."
> Said the Bishop,
> Eating his ketchup:
> "There still remains Eternity
> Swelling the diocese,
> That Elephantiasis,
> The flunkeyed and trumpeting sea."

This poem, she asserts in "Some Notes," "is built on a *scheme* of R's, which in this case produces a faint fluttering sound, like dust fluttering from the ground, or the beat of a dying heart" (italics added). Even the observant may have difficulty assenting to this pattern or "scheme," for at first it seems incontestably hermetic and personally psychologized. It may also be difficult to assent to the critic's conceit of dust emitting a sound. Yet, as before with her work on Pope and Eliot, a close study of her commentary reveals its relevance to the text. Of course, a reader has to accept that an "R" sound gives some suggestion of "faint fluttering," a tenet that perhaps some rigid opponents of affective formalism in criticism may not sanction. It is also important to observe that Sitwell is not so dogmatic as to claim for a particular sound a single, absolute association. Her interpretations, as one would expect of a critic attracted to Coleridge, are all contextual.

The frequency of trilled "r"s in many languages (and even in dialects of English), gives phonetic grounds for believing that "r"s possess a "faint fluttering sound." What follows in her explication is the more questionable part: do "r"s convey the feeling of "dust fluttering from the ground"? The answer, assuredly, is "not necessarily," and it is important to see that this seems to be Edith Sitwell's view also. She writes that the "r" sounds are "like dust fluttering from the ground, or the beat of a dying heart" (italics added), an assertion which demonstrates that, to her, there is no one absolute or definitive association: here it can be that of "dust" or "heart." She abstracts from the aural presence of "r"s only the essential faint beating (the heart is dying) or faint fluttering. The association of heart and dust is supplied, not by the critic solely in a virtuoso improvisation of what John Crowe Ransom might call "psychological affective language," [3] but by the poet who states in this poem that the "dust is everything—the heart to love and the voice to sing." It is the poet's "shuddering" that suggests the critic's "fluttering." The poet's definition of "dust" as "voice" justifies the critic's "sound, like dust." Moreover, this critical conceit of synaesthetic exchange between sight and sound further derives from the disintegration which the whole poem discusses. "Fluttering" appropriately describes both sight and sound.

In this critical writing we find once again, not only the critic's careful scrutiny of the correspondence of meaning and form (sound) that we assume to be the function of art (whether we can demonstrate it or not), but since the critic here is the poet, we also see evidence of at least the intention of meaningful order and design in Dame Edith's poetry.

In continuing to explicate "Said King Pompey" and remarking in "Some Notes on My Poetry" that "In the first two lines, the sound rises" (p. xix), Sitwell forces the reader to reconsider the poem with an experiencing ear. In this demand there is perhaps no difficulty, for the sounds do "rise" (by any phonetic description): the first line moves from "said" to "ape" and the second from "shuddering" to "cape." Moreover, each element or section (there appears to be a caesura after "Pompey" and "black") of these two lines "rises." In fact, the phonetic sensation of "rising" is present in each foot and is reinforced in the stress of all but three of the feet.

> Said King/Pompey//the em/peror's ape//
> Shudder/ing black//in his tem/poral cape//

This is straightforward enough, but one may indeed ask why we should have to learn that the sound "rises"? Is this not another example of the gratuitous personal association which appears to characterize so much of Sitwell's criticism and poetry?

If the reader has understood (if not accepted) the critic's initial discovery of the appropriateness of the poem's sound (its "r" "scheme") to the poem's subject (the "shuddering" of "dust"-"heart"), he knows that he must correlate the language and terms of Sitwell's criticism closely to those of the poetry. "Rising" sound then may appear relevant, because the poem discusses "shuddering" or "fluttering," one aspect of which is a "rising" one. More importantly, perhaps, we note that the poem ends with "Eternity swelling the diocese" and the sea an "elephantiasis." A poet and critic of Sitwell's organic persuasion might well endeavor to construct and comment on a "rising" sound to complement the "rising" sense.

We also read in the criticism of this poem that "the poem *deliberately guttered down* into meaninglessness" (italics added). Rising and finally falling, we realize, are appositely remarked and intended in a portrait of one who is "shuddering." That the "falling" dimension of the poem is critically described as "guttered down" is also not without a textual relevance. "To gutter" means "to stream," and in that sense it recalls and is supported by the concluding image of the sea. The attendant meaning of "gutter" as related to the lowly also relates to the ending of the poem with its theme of dissolution and defilement so well embodied in "Acropolis" as evocation of the reduction of everything to rubble and dust. It is also appropriate that while the ending "deliberately guttered down into meaninglessness" the sound of the conclusion (like the opening lines of the poem) rises,

> *The flunkeyed and trumpeting sea.*

Rising and falling make up not only the theme of the poem but also its texture.

This assiduous cultivation of interconnection and her particular use of the term and concept of "shadow" to describe it is well illustrated in her continuing explication (in "Some Notes") of "King Pompey,"

> "Pompey," in sound, is a dark distorted shadow of "Emperor" and of its crouching echo, "temporal"—a shadow upside down, one might say, for in "Emperor" the sound dies down in hollow darkness, whereas in "Pompey" it begins in thick muffling animal darkness and then rises, dying away into a little thin whining air.

Once again there insists a question about the relevance and accuracy of her critical exposition. In what meaningful way, for example, is "Pompey" a "dark, distorted shadow" of "Emperor"?

In coming to terms with Sitwell's conception here we are forced to realize that a shadow can precede the object shadowed; it is the light source that determines the shadow's direction and placement. And, in the context of this poem, a reader may be prepared for this particular inversion of usual order by the syntactical order of "Said King Pompey" which is an inversion of the more usual syntax of "King Pompey said." "Distorted," therefore, may be used to inform us of this inversion.

Significantly, "temporal" is here an "echo" of "emperor," a usage which confirms the observation that, to Edith Sitwell, an "echo" involves similarity: there is little phonetic change and no inversion from "emperor" to "temporal." And it may not be fortuitous here that the "echo" is the word "temporal," for, as I suggested above, "echo" is a term that appears to connote for Sitwell the mutable and dying in time. Her "shadow," embracing more complexity, is used here to describe a "distorted" relationship (but still with meaning) between "Pompey" and "emperor." If this connection were one of close similarity—as with "emperor" and "temporal"—it might also have been an "echo," but there is inversion. The rising sounds of "emperor" and "Pompey" are in opposing positions: "In 'emperor' the sound dies down in hollow darkness, whereas in 'Pompey' it begins in thick muffling animal darkness and then rises." But there is more than phonetic antithesis here. The relationship of "Pompey"-"emperor" is the opposing one of beast and man (analogous to the fall and rise which the poem also documents), an opposition heightened by the irony of the ape's name, "Pompey." The suitability of "shadow" to describe this combination is further confirmed by the permanence of this human condition; it is no fleeting tension, only the ape's *cape* is "temporal."

In the resolution of Sitwell's critical perception we come to understand that "Pompey" is not only a "distorted shadow," but also a "dark" one, because in the poem King Pompey the ape is "shuddering black." Appropriately, it would seem, she remarks an "animal darkness" about the poem. Even the sky, we must remember, is "hairy," and the sea an "elephantiasis."

For further understanding of her impressment of a controlling order upon her work we might ask why "Pompey"

is the "shadow" of "emperor." Why could it not be the
reverse, with "emperor" the shadow of "Pompey"? The
answer seems to be that it could, especially outside of the
poem, but within the poem Edith Sitwell chooses one
interpretation, one order, and that is the one developed
and reinforced by the whole context: the theme of inverse
evolution or dissolution. Moreover, the theme of inverse
evolution logically employs what appears to be the per-
verse order, and the ironic possibilities of that order
should need no explanation. Furthermore, not only, as I
said above, is the subjective or instigating element—in a
sense the prior—placed last in the statement "Said King
Pompey," but the prior comes last in the sequence "Indianapolis"—"Acropolis." Of this juxtaposition Miss Sitwell
writes, "The crazy reversed sound of 'Indianapolis,' 'Acropolis'—'Acropolis' being a hollow darkened echo of 'Indianapolis,' broken down and toppling over into the
abyss—this effect is deliberate." Not only is there a "reversed sound" in this sequence, but also a reversed chro-
nology—as there is in the inverted evolution of the poem
which has the ape ("King Pompey") as the shadow of the
man ("emperor").

Edith Sitwell's comments on the role of "Acropolis"
also further define and illuminate her usage of "shadow"
and "echo." We note here above that, to her, "Acropolis"
is "a hollow darkened echo" of "Indianapolis." But what
is there in the relationship that supports this usage rather
than "shadow"? If the combination "emperor"-"temporal"
was one of "echo," what is there of analogy here? In
searching for a consistency based "upon cause and reason"
in Sitwell's criticism one might now protest that there
does not seem to be the similarity between "Indianapolis"-
"Acropolis" that existed between "emperor"-"temporal"
and which partly determined, in my previous analysis, the
conditions of "echo" as a technical term of her criticism.
Yet here, too, the logic is saved.

The endings ("polis") of each word in the combination
do correspond, but "Indiana" and "Acro" have little connection beyond a kind of reversal in which "Indiana" ends

with "a" and "Acro" begins with it.[4] Here we must note that Sitwell describes this relationship as a *"crazy* reversed sound," and this is an aspect which is appropriately described by "echo." A reversal or connection of a meaningful nature is nonexistent here, and therefore is manifestly "crazy." And sounds that become jumbled and "crazy" can be echoes, for that is an aspect and nature of echoes (as in the Marabar Caves). "Shadows" by the method of their generation cannot be so meaningless or "crazy." Presumably it is with such a logic that we find Sitwell remarking "candle, and its shadow 'black'" (p. xxv) in the lines (from "The Drum").

> *Watch the candles lit by fright*
> *One by one through the black night.*

Here the relationship "candle"-"black" can be analyzed: the shadow ends with the sound with which its source began, and its beginning has the "l" sound with which "candle" ends. That there are other witty observations possible on this combination further attests to the nature of Sitwell's usage of "shadow" as opposed to "echo."

The informing presence of the author and her deliberate effects is continually manifested in the poet's own explication of "Said King Pompey." She tells us that "since the circumstances of the world have changed" she has come to change the ending of the poem. In the revised version the Bishop, no longer "eating his ketchup" says,

> *The world is flat . . .*
> *But the see-saw crowd sent the Emperor down*
> *To the howling dust—and up went the Clown*
> *With his face that is filched from the new young Dead;*
> *And the Tyrant's ghost and the Low-Man-Flea*
> *Are emperor brothers, throw shades that are red*
> *From the tide of blood (Red Sea, Dead Sea),*
> *And Attila's voice or the hum of a gnat*
> *Can usher in eternity.*

"Frivolous" aspects like the ketchup have been replaced, "since the circumstances of the world have changed from the moronic-cackling of the 1920's over ruin, over their bright-coloured hell, to a naked menace, where the only bright colour is that of blood." Yet much remains of the poem's central tone as announced in its first part (unchanged). And assuming that Sitwell is as careful of organic structure as she seems to be in her criticism much would have to be the same or she would have had to rewrite the opening section. We note that the sea imagery of "tide of blood" and the phrase "usher in eternity" still support the sense and sound of "rise" as anticipated in the poem's opening lines. "See-saw" . . . "down" . . . "up went" also reinforce her earlier analysis.

Continuing to exhibit her interest in connection I might here point out that in the sequence "Red Sea, Dead Sea" meaning is qualified by a rhyming (that is, connecting) juxtaposition. In the revised conclusion of "Said King Pompey" the "Tyrant's ghost and the Low-Man-Flea" cast "shades," a choice of term that may be significant because what is conveyed through these "shades" is aural sound—"Attila's voice or the hum of a gnat"—which topically might be more associated with "echoes." However, considering the length of time that thematically must be bridged in the poem's statement, and considering Sitwell's demonstrable association of "echo" with the temporal and dying, her choice of a cognate of "shadow" is understandable. In this poem it is the duration, the evolution of "naked menace," the generation of Ape-Tyrant that is shocking, and especially so in the revised version.

This special affinity of "shadow" and its cognate "shade" with what is substantial and enduring is particularly remarked in Sitwell's analysis of her poem "The Bat" (p. xxi).

It is admissible that certain arrangements of words ending in "ck" ("black," "Quack," "duck," "clack," etc.) cast little, almost imperceptible shadows. In "The Bat," a poem about the waiting, watching world of the Shade, I have contrasted these shadows, so small yet so menacing, with those flat and shadeless words that end with "t" and with "d". . . . In this poem, some of the "a"s and the "u"s have neither depth nor body, are flat and death-rotten; yet at times the words in which they occur cast a small menacing shadow because of the "ck" endings, though frequently these shadows are followed almost immediately by flatter, deader, more shadeless words.

In her further commentary on this poem she mentions that the "small menacing shadows" (which the word "mountebank" casts) "prophesy of the ultimate darkness," a remark which not only associates shadow with a kind of permanence, but also anticipates the exposition of "Shadow" as a central symbol of her poetry. Continuing to note her association of shadow with the vital and organic she writes of "The Drum" that "In the lines,

> Clatter and quack
> To a shadow black

. . . it is a fact that the second syllable of 'clatter,' instead of casting a shadow, shrinks away into itself and dies" (p. xxiv).

Although Edith Sitwell does use "echo," and occasionally in what seems to be a synonomous usage with "shadow," she is demonstrably less interested in the effect of causal sequence to which "echo" pertains than in that of symbolic correspondences to which "shadow" belongs. The phenomenon of serial effect in no way sponsors the complex vision of simultaneity and substantial relationship that "shadow" does. I find, by count of the critical terms in "Some Notes on my Poetry" that she uses "shadow" twenty-four times and "echo" only thirteen. ("Mirror" occurs three times.) Moreover, if these instances of "shadow" are added to the fourteen related usages of "shade," the special importance of "shadow" is evident.

In her *Poet's Notebook* Edith Sitwell cites Poincaré's statement, ". . . the accident of a rhyme calls forth a system from the shadow," and even appends, "And a whole planetary system" (p. 31). With or without benefit of rhyme she describes and establishes what appears to be a system—a symbolist order—dependent on "shadows."

Rejecting what is "flat," of single vision, "dead" or shadowless; mindful always, as her revision of "Said King
Pompey" indicates, of the real world and its substantial
complexities, she appears to be particularly involved with
the many systemic implications of "shadow."

WHEN EDITH SITWELL speaks of the system generated by the connective aspect of "shadow" of sound, she is, apparently, speaking about the organization of a single poem. For although as a critic she makes many demands of the reader who would follow her explication of a poem's unity, she does not do what indeed would seem to be the impossible: to describe the continuation of intricate aural patterns beyond one poem. And in assessing the nature of her criticism it is important to see that she does not propose such an extreme commitment.

Yet in remarking this limit it is well to consider that Edith Sitwell's demonstrated interest in the aural vitality of a single poem does not necessarily mean that she neither recognizes nor possesses other organic connection between poems. A dedication such as she has to the organic autonomy of a single poem does not preclude some relationship of that single poem with its environment including other poems, "No organism, including an organic poem, can exist apart from an environment." [1] When we speak of autonomy as "organic" we make an important qualification: no living entity can be absolutely independent.

Edith Sitwell's chief interest as a critic is the aural nature of a poem, and this explains why the emphasis and bulk of her criticism is on the structure of single poems. Moreover, she has expressed awareness of this emphasis in *The Pleasures of Poetry* where she tells us that "The technical notes which follow are less concerned with the structure than with the texture of poems." [2] Even so, she has not been completely silent on the relationships among poems. For example, she writes of Eliot, in *Aspects of Modern Poetry*, that "In the opening lines of 'Gerontion,' . . . I think we have a version of the theme inspiring the lines [from *The Waste Land*]

> *There I saw one I knew, and stopped him, crying:*
> *Stetson!*
> *You who were with me in the ships at Mylae!*

And that Sitwell believes this connection is useful to the reader is clear from the way she introduces that remark (p. 119),

> "Gerontion" is one of the greatest and most significant of Mr. Eliot's poems, and though, for once, I find myself in accordance with Dr. Leavis, inasmuch as I am embarrassed for the fear of insulting the reader's intelligence—I hope I shall be forgiven for tracing a connection I believe to exist between the opening of this, and the closing of "The Burial of the Dead" in "The Waste Land."

Elsewhere in "Gerontion" it is meaningful to Sitwell that "the rain for which the old man is waiting has the same significance as that of the water in 'What the Thunder Said'—the last section of 'The Waste Land'" (p. 120). We note that Sitwell does not develop very carefully her perceived relationship between "Gerontion" and *The Waste Land*. Typically, her exposition is "tracing" and something less than satisfactory exegesis. But of her awareness of connection between poems there is no doubt.

Her remarks on the inter-relationship of Shakespeare's sonnets are particularly instructive. "It is to my feeling, desecration," she writes in the introduction to one of her anthologies, "to separate the sonnets, and to take them from their exact place. The pattern is broken—the Parthenon is in ruins." [3] The esthetic conscience that would not separate Shakespeare's sonnets—commonly taken "out of context" by even the most rigorous adherents to organic criticism—is indeed a scrupulous one. When in the same introduction, she quotes Coleridge on "the power of reducing multitude into unity" (p. 16), she obviously is not speaking solely of the unity achieved within a single poem. It is her unremitting dedication to the concept of a "Parthenon" that informs our reading of her most recent statement, in her introduction to *Music and Ceremonies* (1963), that

> the poems in this book are those written since the publication of my *Collected Poems* and will eventually form a part of my collected work.

It is apparently with this kind of meaningful collection in mind that she has said of an earlier publication,

> The poems in *The Song of the Cold* are now arranged in the sequence to which they belong. For instance, "Gold Coast Customs" obviously sprang from the same impulse as did the poems in *Street Songs*.[4]

As I shall have the occasion again to remark below, she has not placed all of her poems within her collected work. Those that are, however, quite clearly in the estimate of the poet-critic herself contribute to a unity "reduced" from the multiplicity of individual poems. That she is a poet of collection, intellection, and of deliberate esthetic is a position already suggested by much of her criticism and is a view that will be increasingly supported in this study.

In the same introduction in which she says that her new poems shall eventually form a part of her "collected work," Edith Sitwell states that "since the publication of my *Collected Poems* I have moved, technically, in different ways." But it is important to note that these "different ways" are not directions to isolate her latest work from the previous. In fact, as she continues to say, "Now I am an old woman, I remember those lessons learned in my early days." There is, as she remarks, a noticeable return to an earlier style of shorter line, but this is not to say that there is no continuous connecting element of theme or imagery extending from her earliest to her latest work, including what now, by her own comments, seems to be her "middle" period.

What she remarks in her latest preface is that in her early work, "In *Façade*, for instance, the poems often warmed themselves at fantastical fires and danced in the light of glow-worms." Now, in 1963 she remembered that "Poetry should always be running on pleasant feet, sometimes swift, sometimes slow." Thus, we might expect to find her latest poetry different from the slow-moving, burdened long line of what now may be her extensive "middle" period, the time between 1940 and 1953 when her utterance in a world of war and nuclear fission was largely elegiac in tone and movement. In examining the thirteen poems of *Music and Ceremonies* we indeed find the tone different from *Three Poems of the Atomic Age* (1949). The newer poems are less directly engaged, less expansively majestic, but the themes are much the same as titles like "The Outcasts," "March Past," and "The War Orphans" from the new collection indicate.

Study of the new poems confirms the observation that if the poet has to comment on the return to an earlier technical mode, there need be no such statement for the informing mind and spirit; they are continuous.

"The Outcasts" (1962), the initial poem of her last collection of poetry,[5] opens with

> *This is the night-moment when the Damned*
> *Rejected by pools that slake the thirst of*
> > *beasts of prey,*
> *Creep in the rags of their hearts to Judas.*

A new style? A return to "lessons learned in my early days"? Here are lines from "A Song of the Dust," not a poem of her "early days" but of her "middle" days, of ten years previously.

> *And on the great roads of Night*
> *The unseen suns are singing of their triumph.*
> *All things lie in the clime of Man's forgiveness.*
> *Oh, tell me not we are face to face with our own dust—*
> *That Judas creeps, night-long, from each crevice*
> > *like the spring,*
> *Only to meet Judas and again Judas!*

The poem from which these lines are taken is of considerable length—some eighty lines—whereas the recent one is only twelve, and many of the older poem's are long,

> *That Judas creeps, night-long, from each crevice*
> *like the spring,*

Yet, although the line compared with the recent one,

> *Creep in the rags of their hearts to Judas*

is longer and one does indeed feel a sparer spirit about the recent work, there is at least one long line (hexameter) in "The Outcasts,"

> *Rejected by pools that slake the thirst of*
> *beasts of prey.*

And obviously no line, even the shortest ones,

> *The moment of the year*
> *When comes a drop of mercy to those lips*
> *That kissed but to betray*
> *'O brother, pity me!*
> *One drop, only one drop!' No answer came.*
> *They crept away,*

is read with the speed and élan of those from a poem of "the early days" like "Trio for Two Cats and a Trombone" (*Façade*, 1922).

> *The*
> *Trumpet and the drum*
> *And the martial cornet come*
> *To make the people dumb—*
> *But we*
> *Won't wait for sly-foot night.*

What is striking to a reader of a "middle" poem like "Song of the Dust" and a "late" or "last" poem such as "The Outcasts" is the continuity of imagery in the reworking of Judas, the presence of Night, the mode of creeping, even the similarity of "night-moment" and "night-long." Since the author herself states in her introductory remarks that her new poems "will eventually form a part of [her] collected work," it is hard not to respond to obvious relationships between poems like "Song of the Dust" and "The Outcasts." Reading them as parts that have been collected, one finds the presence of one within the other, and new dimensions of depth are added to our reading.

One perception that seems significant from such an interpretation is the difference between the possibility of mercy in this world (as pleaded in "Song of the Dust") and the denial in Hell (as affirmed in "The Outcasts"). The ironic and incisive description of the damned in "The Outcasts,"

> They crept away
> To their hell that is the Dead Sea Shore. Their bliss,
> Their love, they knew now was a Pillar of Salt,
> From whom they had hoped to win Oblivion's Kiss,

is thus skillfully qualified by the presence of the previous poem. Furthermore, the poem may be fully understood only when it is seen to be a careful combination of the curt and cold rejection of the damned in Sydney Goodsir Smith's "Defeat O' the Hert" [6] from which Sitwell takes her poem's epigraph, and in which poem "The strauchle's dune" (the "struggle's done"). It is important to see that in Dame Edith's work the struggle may not be done, and that it may not be done is partly because in her previous poem to which she returns for imagery, the plea is made,

> Oh, tell me not we are face to face with our own dust—
> That Judas creeps, night-long, from each crevice
>   like the spring,
> Only to meet Judas and again Judas!

The reassurance of love, even for a Judas, is then given, for

> There is another Who has shed all but the thunder's glory,
> All but the heart of dust.

The song of this dust speaks not of the heart's defeat, as does Smith's poem, but of how

> *morning comes to the heart, and the*
> > *heart's warmth, its fevers,*
> *Rapacity and grandeur—comes to the dress*
> *Of flesh inconstant as the splendors and the rubies*
> *Of the day's hear, the pity and glory of the rainbow.*

A reading of the new poem informed by the larger design of which Sitwell makes it a part (by epigraph and recollecting imagery) indeed makes "The Outcasts" in its tensions between various forces a poem in which no struggle is yet definitively completed.

"March Past," the second poem of the late collection, can be similarly compared to "The Song of the Dust." The late poem opens with

> *In this August of the world, amidst the auguries,*
> *And auspices of whispering dust,*
> *The increase of honor and of Dives' honey,*
> *And the green seeds of predestination lying*
> *Under the almond husk of what was once the world,*

a passage which recalls and may be compared with the one of a decade earlier.

> *Who knows which dust is Dives, which black dust*
> *Is Lazarus, changed into garden loam*
> *To await the fertile universal will?*
> *For does not the dust of the common world hold*
> > *the dark seed*
> *Of a humble plant that grows. . . .*

The earlier poem is more discursive and contains lines that are longer than any one of the twenty in "March Past." There is more formal certainty in the more recent one, and in this is quite rightly compared by the author to the "technical exercises" of *Façade*. Yet again, as with "The Outcasts," there is none of the gaiety ("terrible" or otherwise) that informs much of Sitwell's early work. Our conclusion must offer a necessary adumbration of the poet's critical remarks in her preface. If there is return to the past of *Façade*, as there is, it is a development that takes no violent deviation from the work of her "middle" maturity. If the poetry of her last work changed technically from that of the preceding or "middle" period—as it did to a degree—there nonetheless are other elements of resonance and continuity to observe.

Returning to a point made above, there was no comment by Dame Edith on change other than technical (and even that is not a violent one), because, as this study seeks to demonstrate, the author has, from first to last, made the central course of her poetry a retrospective one of interwoven and recollecting complexity. Her themes and images are continuously worked and reworked, simultaneously new and old in a technique that may now be meaningfully described by her own critical term "shadow." As she herself in analyzing her own and others' poetry describes significant unitive elements as "shadows," so might the critic of her entire body of work usefully employ the term to characterize the connecting elements within her canon. Change is important and is evident in the course of the poetry, but it is change not of an uncontrolled or unintelligible growth, but of process as in the mutations which she describes in "A Song of the Dust,"

> *like the change in the word from*
> *smaragdum to smeraldo,*
> *From emeraude to emerald. . . .*

Just as the late poetry has been made out of the images and themes of the so-called "middle" poetry that body of work in turn has manifestly grown from the early work. Yeats, as well as noting the "necessity of contrast" in her work, also brilliantly perceived that Edith Sitwell

> has . . . exaggerated metaphors into mythology carrying them from poem to poem, compelling us to go backward to some first usage for the birth of the myth.[7]

Yeats, of course, in writing this had only Sitwell's allegedly "early" poetry to judge. His observation of interconnection, then, is possibly less remarkable than if it had been made in 1942 or 1944 when the collections *Street Songs* and *Green Song* appeared and seemed to critics to be inexplicably different from her previous work. Horace Gregory, for example, reviewing these works in 1945 saw in them "a suddenly discovered and unpredictable source of inspiration." [8] But the author herself in her preface to *The Song of the Cold* of that same year wrote that " 'Gold Coast Customs' obviously sprang from the same impulse as did the poems in *Street Songs*." If *Customs* of 1929 and *Street Songs* of 1942 spring from the same source, any claim of new "inspiration" must be qualified to some degree. And Yeats' judgment is confirmed. And interesting arrangement of her own poems by the poet is seen in her collections *Poems New and Old* and *The Song of the Cold* where she places the earlier poem *Gold Coast Customs* after the later ones of *Street Songs*. Apparently the author herself sees a larger measure of homogeneity and unity in her work than many of her "periodical" critics. Yeats' early remarks, however brief, stand to this day as the most perceptive criticism which Sitwell has received.

The summary view that Sitwell's early poetry precedes a sudden new "inspiration" is, however, a persistent and prevailing opinion. J. I. M. Stewart in the most recent of "authoritative" literary histories declares that Edith Sitwell "passed . . . from one sort of poetry, maintained well into maturity, to another sort of poetry of vastly greater scope." [9] Difference there is, and it is necessary to note it. But there is always a tendency in the criticism that stakes out "periods" in an author to find sources or "influences" outside the author. If a "middle" period is of a different "inspiration" (as Sitwell's was found to be) from an "early" period, the tendency is to disregard the "early" in explaining the other (except, of course, as contrast). "Influence hunting" is thereby encouraged. In such a way, perhaps, Gregory finds that "Crashaw . . . alone seems to be her visible predecessor" (p. 154) in *Street Songs* and *Green Song*, and Stewart remarks that

> A poem like the "Shadow of Cain" (1947) shows clearly that it is to a world of feeling largely created by Mr. Eliot that much of this transformation must be due.

"Must" is a strong word, and Mr. Stewart is an assertive critic, but he does not convince. For one thing, he seems to contradict himself on the Eliot-Sitwell influence when he writes that

> Dame Edith Sitwell was born in the year before Mr. Eliot, and she was before him in writing brilliantly polished light verse. She was well behind him in moving away from it.

If Sitwell was before Eliot in "brilliantly polished light verse," perhaps she influenced *him* in that genre! But this is the kind of speculation sponsored by the methodology of "periods" which too readily divides artists against themselves. Some of this criticism, allegedly "organic," would deny to a "body" of poetry the very organic quality that it assiduously emphasizes in the single work or part of that totality. It is relevant here to note that Brooks and Warren in a postscript of 1950 to their *Understanding Poetry* (1938) acknowledge "the relation of the single poem to the whole body of the poet's work," and "often," they state (p. xxii),

> the single poem may be profitably regarded as a mere stanza in the long developing and unfolding poem which is the whole work. For in the work of a serious poet we usually find not many themes but few. Even in a poet of great variety and complication, there is some central concern, some fundamental attitude, from which the richness exfoliates. Once we understand this, we find that one poem serves as a gloss upon the next.

Yeats, perhaps the most "various" of modern poets, is an excellent example of what Brooks and Warren are talking about, for he always thought of his work as "collected" and of a variety only fully meaningful in terms of an overriding unity. Mr. Stewart demonstrates that he is more interested in the relationship of Sitwell to Eliot (and vice-versa) than in Sitwell herself. In the single paragraph (of his seven hundred pages) in which he refers to Edith Sitwell five of the seven sentences link her to other poets, principally Eliot.

Stewart is a more discerning critic of Yeats than of Sitwell (undoubtedly because he devotes a long chapter to him) and does indicate that there can be connection-in-growth within a poet's periods. Writing of Yeats' "Ribh at the Tomb of Baile and Aillinn," one of the "Supernatural Songs" (1935) of his last years, he notes (p. 410) that

> the path to it from the *Baile and Aillinn* of 1902 must be one of the longest ever trodden by poet. Yet the connexion is not entirely confined to the common legendary background . . . the late poem preserves faintly but unmistakably . . . the echo of all that Pre-Raphaelite beauty through which the young Yeats had passed.

His remark that "for the reader familiar with the body of Yeats' poetry there is in this whole poem a richness of implication that places it among his most perfect achievements" (p. 411) well illustrates the recognition of the integrity that is possible within and through a more evident diversity. Mr. Stewart suggestively observes that "Under Ben Bulben" "resumes in less than a hundred octosyllabic lines almost everything [Yeats] has ever said (p. 420). It is this quality of inclusiveness that has been underdeveloped in criticism of Edith Sitwell's poetry.

The "way" has been shown, however, particularly by Yeats himself, perhaps because he saw in Sitwell's work something analogous to his own. For one of the impressive marks of Yeats' criticism is that he saw something besides the "lightness" that Stewart (following others) still finds to be the exclusive characteristic of her early poetry. Yeats sees not just "polished light verse" but poetry of a "double" vision, one aspect of which is "elegant" and "artificial," but the other half, "driven by a necessity of contrast" is a "nightmare vision like that of Webster, of the emblems of mortality." [10] And rather than contrasting her to Eliot he sees the similarity of her persistent image of the bone as analogous to Eliot's usage (but without the allegation or implication of "influence" or derivation).

> A group of writers have often a persistent image. There are "stars" in poem after poem of certain writers of the 'nineties as though to symbolize an aspiration towards what is inviolate and fixed; and now in poem after poem by Edith

Sitwell or later writers are "bones"—"the anguish of the skeleton," "the terrible Gehenna of the bone"; Eliot has:

> No contact possible to flesh
> Allayed the fever of the bone.

Furthermore, Yeats notes that "Eliot and Edith Sitwell have much of their intensity from a deliberate re-moulding or checking of past impulse" (p. xxxii), an observation which recognizes a development in terms of the poet's own work. With only her "early" work at hand Yeats in 1936 understood not only the actual accomplishment but also the future course of Sitwell.

In her last collection, *Music and Ceremonies* (1963), the concluding poem (which bears the title of the collection) ends with these significant lines.

> The small and great complete each other, and the end
> Leads to the beginning, and the beginning
> Leads to the end, said the Man of Emeralds
> Dancing like a wave beneath the bough of Spring.

It is important, in the light of the statement of these lines, that Sitwell's "beginning," her first poem "Drowned Suns" (1913)—quoted above in chapter 1—uses both the images of gems and water. Knowing from the author's criticism her commitment to organic structure, and knowing something already about her repetitive patterns, it may be unwise not to suggest some conscious knowledge of this relationship by the author.

Moreover, there is a meaningful evolution to be observed between these poems. If the relationship between these two poems is purposive, it is not merely to assert the poet's fixation for water and gems. There is a more creative relationship that would better justify the poet's statements that "the end leads to the beginning, and the beginning leads to the end."

The first poem is about death and loss; the last is about birth and growth. But the "beginning" is not a definite acceptance of what is lost; the verbal moods of "the swans . . . within the sunset water . . . gaze," "The moon for ever seeks," and "I seek" all establish continuing action.

Although the speaker finds "but wrecks of love's gold argosies," the statement recognizes the possibilities of those "argosies" and of "suns" that are not "lost." Her beginning does not preclude nor contradict her end, and, in fact, its position of seeking explains her later discovery. Her beginning of search or hope amidst loss may well lead her to the concluding recognition (in "Music and Ceremonies") that there is "no confusion" in

> The ample grandeur of the Earth, and death and birth
> Of seasons.

The vision at the "end" is indeed an "ample" one which accommodates and in a sense completes the "beginning." Further illustration below of "ends" realized from "beginnings" within the poetry will reinforce the hypothesis of this study, that an important function of her poems is (in the phrase of "Music and Ceremonies") to "complete each other."

There is recollection here in "Music and Ceremonies" not only of "Drowned Suns" (and other of her poems to be discussed below) but also quite obviously of Eliot's *Four Quartets*. The tone and statement of the lines I have quoted from Sitwell's late poem are very close to the solemn discursiveness and philosophy of Eliot's work, particularly in the passages containing "In my beginning is my end" ("East Coker") and "What we call the beginning is often the end" ("Little Gidding").

This correspondence brings to mind J. I. M. Stewart's claim, partly examined above, that Sitwell is derivative of Eliot. Does this new example give evidence in support of Stewart? Manifestly not. There is no doubt of the allusion here to the *Quartets*, but it so obvious and emphatic that it may be assumed that Sitwell deliberately intends the allusion to be recognized and used by the reader. And, although it is not the intention of this study to investigate extensively Sitwell's debt to other poets, it is clear from reading her work that aside from the architectonic reordering and "shadowing" of her own poetry (which is my concern) she is also "dependent" to some degree on at least a dozen or so poets including, besides the French Symbolists, Jonson, Donne, Marvell, and as we here note, Eliot. But "dependent" must be used here in Eliot's own well-known sense which defends, perhaps even prescribes, a continuation of tradition by rather direct use of one's literary culture, both past and present. The tradition is indeed to serve the individual talent. To whatever degree Sitwell alludes to Eliot it is done openly so that the reader uses Eliot as Eliot, with all of the allusive relevance of the original context that may accompany the transplanted imagery or feeling. It is within this theory that Eliot himself excuses such a "derivative" poet from plagiarism: the intention is not deception but continuity in further growth.

It requires no profound study of "Music and Ceremonies" to realize how this poem about harmony and music may indeed utilize the *Quartets* for reinforcement. If there are emeralds here in the snow, beneath the wave coloring the very earth, there is good reason for allusion to a work where sapphires mingle with the mud, to employ in extension the complementary vision that unifies the refulgent gem with the homely garlic. Moreover, it is apposite here to know that as early as 1929 in "Metamorphosis" (first version) Edith Sitwell was curious about the contrast of jewels with earth. The informed reader of Sitwell will recall from that poem the "dim-jewelled bones" and

> The topaz, sapphires, diamonds of the bone
> That mineral in our earth's dark mine.

But Sitwell's involvement with Eliot here is only part of the poem's resonant totality. More important as objects for this study are the connecting "shadows" from her own poems which, for example, unite this late poem with others of her own past.

In "How Many Heavens" of *Street Songs* (1942), some twenty years before "Music and Ceremonies," Sitwell is much more discursive and descriptive about the emerald quality of Spring. The poem opens with

The emeralds are singing on the grasses
And in the trees the bells of the long cold are ringing—
My blood seems changed to emeralds like the spears
Of grass beneath the earth piercing and singing.

And immediately the emerald greenness is attributed to God.

God is everything!
The grass within the grass, the angel in the angel, flame
Within the flame, and He is the green shade that came
To be the heart of shade.

We find, in the same poem further association of God and emerald greenness in

God is the stone in the still stone

and

He is the . . . sweet apple's emerald lore.

If in the poet's own statement her last collection is to take its place in her "collected" poems, a previous usage and development of the emerald image cannot be ignored in interpreting another part of her Parthenon. Thus, the earlier poem suggests that the "Man of Emeralds" reference in the late poem may also carry some reference to God or Christ. The association in the later poem may be, of course, with the mythic Green Man, but there is no previous suggestion of that view in the poetry, and analogous development of her other images—her "mythology" in Yeats' reference—would suggest the preference of the religious theme, or, at the very least, the presence of a religious dimension as a complement to the secular myth.

This interaction of her previous work with this poem "Music and Ceremonies" is further illustrated by the relevance of the poem "Holiday" (from *Green Song*, 1944), in which we read

Beneath the flowering boughs of heaven
The country roads are made of thickest gold—
They stretch beyond the world, and light like snow

Falls where we go, the Intelligible Light
Turns all to gold, the apple, the dust, the unripe wheat-ear.

Here is one of the antecedent usages of "the great flowering boughs" of "Music and Ceremonies." Here are the
images of snow and light that open the late poems, "The
emerald lightnings of the snow are gone." The theme of
the earlier poem is the unification of opposites,

> *On this great holiday*
> *Dives and Lazarus are brothers again*
> . . . .
> *And lovers meet their bright Antipodes*
> *. . . they forget their minds' polarity*
> *. . . The least ore of gold*
> *And quality of dust*
> *Holds a vein of holiness.*

And the later poem is clearly about the harmony of heaven
and earth,

The harmony and benevolence of all that lies
Between the earth and the great flowering boughs of the
    spring skies.

It is

> *Music and Ceremonies . . . these*
> *Make the earth and heaven harmonize . . .*
> . . . .
> *. . . give the laws for planting*
> *And budding*
> *. . . said the Man of Emeralds*
> *Dancing underneath the bough.*

The earlier poem, which ends with reference to

Christ Who forgives is—He with the bright Hair—
The Sun Whose Body was spilt on our field to bring us
    harvest,

may therefore contribute the further relevance of Christ
to "the ample grandeur of the Earth" of the later poem.
There is nothing to suggest that her late work revises
radically or repudiates the previous work. In fact, as we

know, this late poem itself reminds the reader that "the small and great complete each other." With such a reading her poem indeed reveals the "realizing structure of symbol" [11] that Jack Lindsay has found in her work—but not without what Ihab Hassan has described as the "active reader participation" [12] that such realization of symbol demands.

The deliberation of the *realized* achievement of "Music and Ceremonies" is especially evident if we consider it in the context of the collection *Music and Ceremonies* in which it follows the poem "Prothalamion."

"Prothalamion" in many ways contributes to the total meaning of "Music and Ceremonies" a meaning quite different from its isolated interpretation. This preceding poem, as a poem about marriage, is a companion and prefiguring work to the succeeding one on harmony and unity. There are many lines that are resonant in similarity,

> *Like . . . the green rainbows of the Spring*
> *. . . . .*
> *Amid the thunders of the rising sap*

of "Ceremonies" recall or are "shadows" of

> *Like the spring rainbow, risen from all growth*
> *The sap and singing*

of the previous work. Both poems open with the birth of lilies; both refer often to music, and both express a similar genesis of hope: in "Music and Ceremonies" "dark are music's springs" while in "Prothalamion" "summer grows from a long-shadowed kiss."

It is this last line especially which reminds us here of the function of "Prothalamion" in the evolution of the meaning not only of itself but of the poem which it precedes and in obvious ways introduces. In its own "shadowing" of a number of previous poems it acts as a typical poem within the Sitwell collection. Not only does it have a meaning in itself but it interacts with other poems. Janus-like it looks forward to "Ceremonies" and backward to others. And the total meaning of "Prothalamion" derived from its own qualifying history of relationships is applicable to its future life within the total or organic meaning of "Music and Ceremonies."

No careful reader who knows the work of Edith Sitwell can read "Prothalamion" without recognizing that the lines,

> Love is all life, the primal law,
> The sun and planets to the husbandman,
> The kernel and the sap; it is the power
> That holds the Golden Rainers in the heaven

recall with unique repetition the opening lines of "Holiday" (of twenty years previously),

> O you, all life, the primal Cause—
> The Sun and Planets to the husbandman,
> The kernel and the sap, the life-blood, flower
> Of all that lives, the Power
> That holds the Golden Rainers in the heaven.

And once recalled, the subsequent explication proves that this unusual kind of repetition is not due to impoverishment of creative ability but to a deliberate desire to bring the earlier poem through its representative fragment to the newer or later one. Just as Sitwell's exegesis of "shadows" within single poems indicates that the full meaning of each element in the context can only be found by a juxtaposition or collection of both, so here within the larger realm of her collected work.

It is not quite correct to say, as does Babette Deutsch that Edith Sitwell has a habit

> of introducing bold images in new settings, repeating old themes with fresh emphasis [making] her work appear like a series of tapestries, some of them patched with fragments from an old fabric.[13]

"Patched with fragments" suggests that Sitwell's repetitive elements are not integrated fully or successfully into their new "setting." The fuller function of these "fragments" and "patches" is not really to be fragmentary at all but to fit into one context together with a meaningful history of former context (or even contexts); as a "shadow" Sitwell's special or representative "fragment" has not only an actual presence but also a creating and woven continuity with its source. Writing to Dorothy Wellesley about his difficulty in choosing poems of Edith Sitwell for his Oxford Anthology, Yeats remarked that she was "very hard to select from, poem is so dependent upon poem. It is like cutting a piece out of a tapestry." [14] His observation well describes the woven rather than patched quality of Sitwell's interdependence.

There is no effort made in "Prothalamion" to conceal the interwoven presence (the "threads" rather than "patch") of "Holiday"—there is so much exact or nearly exact repetition (and, we must not forget, throughout her poetry) that its deliberation cannot be reasonably questioned. And here the presence of "Holiday" brings the dimension of that poem's discursive presentation of Christ first to "Prothalamion" and then in turn to "Music and Ceremonies."

The poet of "Prothalamion" also presents to us "shadows" of other poems that openly and in detail speak of the Christian disposition to life. "Green Song" is recalled in several instances. The lines,

> the secret of how Spring began
> In the young world before the Fall of Man

are almost identical with the later ones,

> like the first spring, when it began
> In the young world before the Fall of Man,

and a key line in each poem (as well as in "Metamorphosis" of 1929) is

> Summer grows from a long-shadowed kiss.

The method of interpreting this technique of recollection is well illustrated by the correspondence of the lines from "Prothalamion,"

> *The calyx of the flower of the world, the spirit*
> *Moving upon the water, the defeat*
> *Of all time's ravages*

with the earlier ones of "Green Song,"

> *O my calyx of the flower of the world, you the*
> *spirit!*
> *Moving upon the waters, the light on the breast of the dove.*

In the "Prothalamion" (of 1962) she writes of "the spirit moving upon the waters," but it is not as definitively the Holy Spirit as it was in the earlier poem, "Green Song," where she added the explicit and informing qualification, "the light on the breast of the dove." The later poem is more allusive and subtle, more ambiguous in the reference to the Holy Spirit as is the later image of "The Man of Emeralds," discussed above.

The recollection of "Metamorphosis" with the line,

> *And summer break from a long-shadowed kiss,*

brings to the treatment of birth and rebirth in this combination of poems the added dimension of the reclamation of the classic and pagan past: "of temples that are gone," "Bacchantes," "Pan's huge forests," "Corydon," "Thisbe, Chloë," "Plato," and "Great Golden Hector." The "immortal Sun . . . Heavenly Love" is invoked to redeem this "crumbling dust," "Death's ruined town" of once glorious antiquity. Lazarus, fittingly, is the most insistent image of the poem. "Green Song" describes man's rebirth in terms of "veridian smells, the green rejoicing," for, the poet "asks" (but confidently omits the question mark), "Are we not all of the same substance/ Men, planets and earth." "Prothalamion" continues in this tradition, but becomes more particular in speaking of British subjects—"The Queens and lilies born of British soil." The poem, understandably, is dedicated "for the Marriage of the Duke and Duchess of Kent." In this cluster of poems the poet "marries" the classical past, nature, man, Lazarus, and English royalty within her Christian vision.

In this process the poet appears to weight her poems with meaning accruing from the past, and this may be why her late poetry is less discursive than the work from 1940 to 1954. She can use the accumulated associations of her past work to augment her later meaning. This technique is present from her very beginnings, but, of course, it is most obvious in her later poetry, for the more work there is behind her, the more possibilities exist for its "shadowed" exploitation. It may be for this reason that there is a new spareness about her last poetry: one notes, for example, that in the related poems which I have discussed immediately above, each later poem is less than half the length of its associated predecessor. It is not that she becomes simpler, thin or "light," but that in the full development of her shadowing technique she can be more subtle and less explicative. The burden of explanation is behind her, in a sense, and in her last poetry she is free to take allusive advantage of her earlier work.

The inter-relationship of Edith Sitwell's poems through repetition not only develops the meaning of individual poems, but the technique also manifests the essential symbolism of all her work: unity within diversity. This deliberate recollection within the canon of Sitwell's poetry may be related to what Stephen Spender calls "the vision of a whole situation." Paraphrasing Spender, two recent editors and critics observe that

> The modern, according to Spender, finds its character by confronting the past and including this confrontation within itself as part of a single total experience. It is more than a cultivation of immediacy, of free or fragmented awareness; it is the embodiment in current imagery of a situation always larger than the present, and as such it is also a containment of the resources and perils of the present by rediscovery of a relevant past.[15]

Already in this discussion of repetition I have presented the two kinds of repetitive technique that Edith Sitwell uses to reduce the multiplicity of her individual poems to the unity of a Parthenon, a "single total experience." The conventional one is that of the recurring image which we associate with many poets, especially the symbolists. Although we have seen some of this technique in "Music and Ceremonies" and its related poems, this method will be more fully developed in a later chapter on the symbolism of "shadow" that is pervasive in Sitwell's poetry. It is her other organizing technique, the one unique to her—the repetition of whole elements—that is the concern of this chapter. The use of the "shadow" to describe this process may here require a note of explanation.

In dealing with the exact repetition of elements, as above with the line "Summer grows from a long-shadowed kiss," found in "Metamorphosis," "Green Song," and "Prothalamion," there is no difficulty in employing the noun "shadow" to designate the repeated element or to use the verb or verbal form for the technique. Sitwell's unique method, as I mentioned before, reasonably deserves its own special critical term, in this case, one conveniently of her own critical vocabulary. But there is clearly no advantage in using "shadow" to describe her more conventional employment of recurring imagery, as, for example, in her continual usage of "green" with its universal associations. Difficulty arises, however, (as a reader may have already detected in my discussion of "Music and Ceremonies") when a repeated element is altered to some degree. The question is, after what degree of change is it no longer useful to call a repetition a "shadow"? It will be helpful, perhaps, to a reader to know that I shall employ "shadow" whenever, in my judgment, the extent of the repetition may be considered "unconventional." Hopefully, the usefulness of the critical term will not be greatly impaired by the possibility of disagreement among readers as to what "unconventional" may mean. The necessary critical discrimination may at least have the beneficial effect of increasing our understanding of literary repetition of all kinds.

A study of Edith Sitwell's work continually reveals how aware she was of what she reused from her past. Even in her prose criticism she reveals an exact and conscious control over her material. In *Aspects of Modern Poetry* she says, "Writing of Shelley's lyrics in 'The Pleasures of Poetry' Volume II I said . . ." (p. 87). In discussing Hopkins in *Aspects* she reminds us, "As I said in my first volume of 'The Pleasures of Poetry'. . ." (p. 66). In the chapter on her brother Sacheverell's poetry she remembers that "Writing of a certain vowel scheme in 'Lycidas' I said . . ." (p. 144). Again in *Aspects* on Sacheverell she tells us, "This, as I said in the introduction to the first volume of my Pleasures of Poetry . . ." (p. 158).

Whatever is important to Sitwell may be seen to be kept alive and developed, and as we might expect from one committed to the intricately organic esthetic which she has revealed in her own criticism, she endeavors to foster a poetic growth analogous to that which attends life. She writes in the introduction ("Some Notes on my Poetry") to her *Collected Poems* that "Technically, I would come to a vital language—each word possessing an infinite power of germination" (p. 6), and one can indeed discover the embodiment of this "growth of consciousness" (p. xxxiii) in her style. For example, what would we make of this obvious repetition of lines in two adjacent poems of *Green Song*? In "Girl and Butterful" we read

We stare at the young girl chasing a yellow butterfly
On the summer roads that lead from Nothing to Nowhere.

What golden racers, young winds, have gone!

and in the next poem, "Green flows the river of Lethe—O," we find

And the young girls were chasing their hearts like the gay
*   butterflies*
Over the fields of summer—
O evanescent velvets fluttering your wings
Like winds and butterflies on the Road from Nothing to
*   Nowhere!*

The repetition is extensive and unique enough, I believe, to warrant the term "shadow." As with many of her "shadows" it may even be too insistent for some tastes—but there is, however, no question about its use "upon cause and reason." Comparison of the poems seems to be intended, for they are physically brought together in the collection. And the result of the enforced collation is to enrich each poem. The question with which the first poem ends,

> are Asia, Africa and Cathay
> But golden flowers that shine in the fields of summer
> As quickly dying?

is answered by the second poem, but the presence of the first poem plays a part in that answer. All things indeed do die a physical death — not quickly, but surely, and there is a sense of loss in that death. Yet the very act of physical death brings about the possibility of a kind of regeneration, that of the spirit, that of memory. "Lethe," Sitwell forces us to recall, is not just the water of the dead, it is the water from which the dead drink before reincarnation. That is why "Lethe," for Sitwell, is "green"; within it are growth and life.

The act of memory is a reincarnation for this poet. When in "Lethe," in the second poem of the "set," she describes the remembered dresses of the young girls, "those golden racers" of "Girls and Butterfly" as "evanescent velvets," she subtly shows them to be something more than "evanescent" by the continuing life of the imagery from poem to poem. The technique restores, regenerates and tends to arrest time, a process fitting to the assertion of these poems that

> long is the terrible street of the Blood
> . . . .
> It stretches for ever. . . .

This unique structural affirmation of regeneration and permanence is a method analogous to that which Sitwell praises in Le Corbusier's work wherein "unity of idea . . . reaches from the unity of the materials used to the unity of the general contour." [16]

No explication of the presence and purpose of Edith Sitwell's "shadowing" technique is as effective as that of her *Five Variations on a Theme* (1933), which consists of

"Romance," "Two Songs" ("Come, My Arabia," and "My desert has a noble sun for heart"), "Metamorphosis," and "Elegy on Dead Fashion." Such a collection is explicit presentation of a unity made up of multiplicity, that all five variations are needed to express her total view of the theme or are in some way relevant to the theme's exposition. It is difficult to believe that the poet deliberately grouped together for publication in this special way superfluous or tautological pieces.

The theme of the five assembled (or "collected") poems is the defeat of inexorable Time "That is the conqueror of our green clime." Her subject is "dark Time" that

> *conceives to fill his grave*
> *Devouring the last faith, the word love gave*

and which leaves even Venus "blackened, noseless, old" to endure

> *The terrible Gehenna of the bone*
> *Deserted by the flesh, tears changed to stone.*

But her theme is that there is relief or consolation to be found among the "crumbling dust" of "Death's ruined town." She asks, in "Romance,"

> *Grieves*
> *This empire of green shade when honeyed rains*
> *And amber blood flush all the sharp green veins*
> *Of the rich rose?*

The answer in this description of a time of love's fulfillment is obvious, but it contains in "grieves" the warning of the impending disabling toll of Time. The lines also contain the conceit by which the ravage of Time shall be conquered. In these poems, as in all of Sitwell's, the poetic sensibility laments the isolated and deserted or loveless state and celebrates the connecting and enduring devotions of love both physical and spiritual. Her symbols of the fruitful life are connective: organic as the rose with veins and visiting blood, or hierarchical and unitive as "empire."

Here in this passage, and repetitively throughout these five (and other) poems, the blood is "amber" to connote a state of permanence, but permanence within flux. Here, in the three long poems the "empire" is of "green shade" which recollects from these various poems the possibilities of growth from darkness. Just as Lethe River was "green" because it transforms the dead to life, so "shade" can be "green" with its allusive ambiguity of spirit and condition (according to Marvell) of "longer flight." "Shade" connotes a relationship between light and darkness, and in affirming the simultaneous presence of light with darkness the image enables the poet to declare in "Metamorphosis" that

> *grass shall sing*
> *From loveless bones in some foreshadowed spring,*
>
> *And summer break from a long-shadowed kiss.*

In this poet's work it is only by recognizing the "empire of eternal shade" that the manifold terrors of the fleeting present can be vanquished, for under the imaginative disposition of the poet's mind no thing or person need be dead or deserted, nor in this "Metamorphosis" is any future change not possibly "foreshadowed,"

> *Since all things have beginnings; the bright plume*
> *Was once thin grass in shady winter's gloom.*

The supreme terror, as given in this poem is to be apart from growth and relationship, to see only "Death's ruined town and mumbling crumbling dust." In "Elegy on Dead Fashion" she denounces the "unremembering crater of the heart" and "our mountain-high forgetfullness . . . piled above the Dead" who are waiting

> *for some remembered tread*
> *Upon this rock bound march that all we made*
> *To the eternal empire of the shade.*

This collection of variations on a theme is important in a study of Edith Sitwell not only because it shows her purposive commitment to multiplicity or variety within a framework of some unifying aspect, not only because it reveals that dark Time's oblivion and desertion is to be defeated by reviving relationships of love, but also because this constellation of poems demonstrates her supporting technique of recollection among the poems. Here we clearly see her technique of reviving or incorporating one poem within another through "shadowing" to achieve her peculiar quality of "collected work." And one of the most important of her resonating lines is the concluding one of the last quotation above, "empire of shade."

Sitwell's poetic universe, a microcosm of which might be *Five Variations on a Theme*, is well described by this phrase in statement and in function within the poems. Although it does not appear in the two short songs (each of which is only nine lines) it occurs with slight variation in each of the three long poems as well as the second version of "Metamorphosis" written much later in 1946. "Romance" has "this vast empire of green shade," "Metamorphosis" (1929) uses "this vast empire of eternal shade," and "Elegy on Dead Fashion" incorporates "the eternal empire of the shade." Out of context the phrase vaguely describes some kind of permanence; within the poems it has the more specific meaning of an abiding unity that overrides continuous change, a meaning partly given by the element's own recurrence. But the repetition of the similar phrase is not for its own sake exclusively as Babette Deutsch implies in calling it a "patch." The technique binds whole poems together; the presence of a part of one poem within another, acting as a "shadow," asserts not only its own meaning but is witness to the existence of an "external" source that is thematically as well as structurally relevant to the new context.

Five Variations on a Theme supports this consideration of shadows extended throughout the poetry by revealing in each poem an aspect of the central theme that is independently meaningful and also capable of enlarging by complementation the other "companion" pieces. "Elegy on Dead Fashion" emphasizes the "Echoes of elegances lost and fled," and recalls by such lines as

> *Queen Thetis wore pelisses of tissue*
> *Of marine blue, or violet, or deep blue,*

> *Beside the softest flower-bells of the seas.*
> *In winter, under thick swan-bosomed trees,*

specifically and meaningfully the artificial world of *Façade*
where in "Waltz" we found

> *By Queen Thetis*
> *Pelisses*
> *Of tarlatine blue.*

"Elegy" is not a poem of achieved consolation. It recognizes "this rock-bound march"

> *To the eternal empire of the shade*

but shrinks from confronting the "most loving Dead" lest
they "know us more dead" and "weep." As yet the "empire of shade" is not "green" and, although the poem's
speaker knows the terror of living "each in his accustomed
grave, alone," the poem presents only a mood of search for
a harmony sought but not fully understood or realized.

"Metamorphosis" (first version, three years after
"Elegy") presents, as the title indicates, the possibility of
change, and the lament of "Elegy" is transformed into a
more confident assertion of reconcilement with a life that
knows the "anguish of the skeleton deserted by the flesh."
The change appears to be mainly a religious one, for
although in "Elegy" there had been a reference to Lazarus, it is not until this poem that a hope of consolation is
manifested.

> *Then my immortal Sun arose, Heavenly Love,*
> *To rouse my carrion to life and move*
>
> *The polar night, the boulder that rolled this,*
> *My heart, my Sisyphus, in the abyss.*
>
> *Come then, my Sun, to melt the external ice*
> *Of death, and crumble the thick centuries,*
> *Nor shrink, my soul, as dull wax owlish eyes*
> *In the sun's light, before my sad eternities.*

"Romance" (1933), a poem about love and its loss, is an
interesting variation on the theme of this collection,
which is the burden of finding a harmony within and

despite the flux of Time. It is interesting, because from the sequence of "Elegy" and "Metamorphosis" one might assume that the poet is undergoing a facile process of attaining a certitude, which at the conclusion of "Metamorphosis" was clearly Christian. "Romance," another variation of four years later, indicates the persistent ravage of loss and abandonment, and presents no consoling religious solution, at least no overt one. Her technique of "shadowing" is here especially important.

The poem concludes with three stanzas depicting the melancholic loss of a lover.

> So winter fell; the heart shaped like the rose
> Beneath the mountain of oblivion lies
> With all death's nations and the centuries.
> And this song ending fades like the shrill snows,
>
> Dim as the languid moon's vast fading light
> That scatters sparkles faint and dim and chill
> Upon the wide leaves round my window sill
> Like Aethiopia ever jewelled bright . . .
>
> So fading from the branches the snow sang
> With a strange perfume, a melodious twang
> As if a rose should change into a ghost—
> A ghost torn to a perfume on the leaves.

The image of "Aethiopia ever jewelled bright" is one that attracts our attention, for it does not complete one's expectations from "winter fell" and the "moon's vast fading light." Apparently, if we can judge from the metaphoric presentation of this "oblivion," it is a special kind, which has ironically in its "dim . . . fading light" a vision of bright darkness, of "Aethiopia ever jewelled bright." This is particularly remarkable because in the stanza preceding these three concluding ones the poet appears to describe her state as one of "polar night." Or has she? Let us examine the stanza.

> How should I dream that I must wake alone
> With a void coffin of sad flesh and bone:—
> You, with the small undying serpent's kiss,
> You, the dull rumor of the dust's renown—

The polar night, a boulder rolling down
My heart, you Sisyphus, to that abyss
Where is nor light, nor dark, nor soul, nor heart to eat—
Only the dust of all the dead, the sound of passing feet.

The lines,

> *The polar night, a boulder rolling down*
> *My heart, your Sisyphus, to that abyss*

should be familiar, for we have just read them in a slightly different version in the conclusion of "Metamorphosis." And this conjunction indeed establishes a riddling irony, for in that context we find the lines qualified by a "Heavenly Love" which has moved the boulder of Sisyphus. And the lines which follow these in "Metamorphosis" are an invocation for the continued inspiration and sustenance of Christ. Since it seems incredible that a reader could read these two poems "collected" in the same small volume and not be aware of the repetition, again it is reasonable to accept the situation as deliberate. Its purpose, one might understandably conclude, is to qualify each context with the other, just as the repetition of other elements elsewhere in her poems appears to do. The result is that in "Romance" we have the anguish of loss qualified by the remembrance that a similar burden was once informed by a Christian consolation. And conversely, of course, the poem of religious consolation in this extended context is qualified by the actuality of sorrow. The ironic presence of "Aethiopia ever jewelled bright" supports the possibility that there is some illumination here, as does the absence of a question mark in the important stanza beginning "How should I . . ." The allusion by "shadow" to the succor of "Heavenly Love" may also indicate why the concluding stanza of "Romance," although topically of loss, speaks of its melody and "perfume."

> *So fading from the branches the snow sang*
> *With a strange perfume, a melodious twang*
> *As if a rose should change into a ghost—*
> *A ghost turn to a perfume on the leaves.*

"Two Songs," although employing a number of recurrent images and symbols in the presentation of their variations of the theme, do not repeat any unconventional degree of element—an almost exact line or lines—as the other three poems do. And the reason for this may be that their brevity would not support such a practice. Both of these short poems have been excluded by the author from her *Collected Poems*, and, in the light of the nature of their companion poems in this volume (*Five Variations*) it is suggestive to hypothesize that the reason may be that they are, in fact, not as "collected" as the others. Both deal, however, with the metamorphosis that is possible from the waste and desert. "Come my Arabia" describes the splendor that may come from the "Phoenix pyre" of the desolate heart; "My desert has a noble sun for heart" insists that "sad time" shall not triumph, because the poet has "still a noble sun for heart." And these concerns are recognizably the theme of the whole collection: that love in its work of memory and connection redeems all, the lost, the sad, and the desolate.

Five Variations on a Theme stands as a paradigm of the kind of intricate unity that Sitwell achieves among poems, the acute awareness (which she in turn forces upon her readers) of the relationships of her poems to each other. This discipline of Edith Sitwell's goes beyond the recognizable consistency of tone and imagery (which she also possesses) that perhaps every genuine poet exhibits in his work. We know Hopkins for his particular energy of phrasing, for a kind of epithet: we recognize that the poet of

> *The world is charged with the grandeur of God,*
> *It will shine out like shook foil*

is the poet of "plough down sillion shine." The Dylan Thomas of "The force that through the green fuse drives the flower" is clearly the poet of "Heads of the characters hammer through daisies." We find, for example, in Thomas the recurrence of a symbol like "fox" or "moon," and we can compare meaningfully the usage and contexts of

> *The stuffed lung of the fox twitch and cry Love*

with

> *the foxes on the hills barked clear and cold,*

or

> *In the moon that is always rising*

with

> *When only the moon rages.*

There is no doubt that an understanding of "After the Funeral" contributes to a better reading of "Fern Hill." What is less certain with Thomas and other poets—as compared with Edith Sitwell—is that the poet himself has used (and intends his reader to use) certain poems for the full understanding of others. Each poet—or each satisfactory poet—possesses one world, "each hath one, and is one," but few demand the degree of unifying recollection that Edith Sitwell appears to do.

When we read in Sitwell's "Praise We Now Great Men" (*Music and Ceremonies*),

> *Praise we these earthly gods—*
> *Praise with the trumpet's purple sound—*
> *Praise with the trumpet flower*
> *And with that flower the long five-petalled hand*
> *That sweeps the strings,*

and then, in the next poem, on the facing page,

> *Yet still great flowers like violet thunder break*
> *In air, and still the flower of the five-petalled senses*
> *Is surely ours,*

we can hardly discount the insistence of the two uses of "still" in the second poem. Given the repetition of "purple sound" in "violet thunders" and the "shadow" of "that flower the long five-petalled hand" in the "flower of the five-petalled senses," it is difficult not to conclude that the time governed by "still" includes that of the preceding poem, "His Blood Colours My Cheek."

This continuity of the poems, established by "still" and

the "shadow" of "that flower the long five-petalled hand," is evident from the opening lines of "His Blood" which are a kind of reply and counter-statement to the conclud- ing lines of "Great Men." The prior work, as its title may indicate, is a secular devotion; it seeks to

> Praise with our last breath
> These earthly Gods,

and it kindles in its last statement

Fires on the hearth, fires in the skies, fires in the human heart.

This is not the central theme of "His Blood Colours My Cheek" (as again the title may suggest), yet the initial lines of this succeeding poem,

His Blood colours my cheek.
Ah! Were but those Flames the tongue wherewith I speak

seem to continue—as kind of counter-statement—from the previous poem's conclusion. If there are fires of the hearth and human heart which elicit our praise of great men, there are, we subsequently learn, other flames, those of "Christ's Blood," also to consider and praise.

Importantly, we note here that the poet is not repudiat- ing the previous poem. It "still" has its single and auton- omous meaning. It "still" possesses its integrity and has not been suppressed by the second poem. But the state- ment which the poet is beginning to formulate with the opening lines of "His Blood" adds to the previous poem's revelation. This is why the use of "still" is important. Even though the speaker knows the presence of Christ and the Holy Spirit, she insists "surely" that there remain

> still great flowers like the violet thunders break
> In air, and still the flower of the five-petalled senses

—that is, all the grandeur and *human* greatness praised in the first poem. There *still* exist

The sound of violins
And the clear sound of flutes

the just—
Who are not come to judge, but bless

Those who can raise
Gold spirits of men from the rough Ape-dust, and who see
The glory, grandeur hidden in small forms

those
Who bring the morning light
To the hearts of men.

Granting and keeping all this, the second poem nonetheless goes on to illustrate the relative smallness of the
world's passion and greeds,

> *the new world of rulers, the snub-nosed, the vain*
> *and the four-handed,*
> *Building a new Babel for the weak*
> . . . .
> *Over the grave where the heart of Man is laid.*

A reader of the two poems realizes that although man is
capable of great things and merits the praise of the poet's
first poem, yet without the sustenance of Christ's compas-
sionate, the all-seeing Eyes which is the news of the second poem, man is too prone to "primal night." The
"Ape-dust" clutched by the "somnambulist upon the
tight-rope stretched over nothingness" in the poem "His
Blood Colours My Cheek" recalls and qualifies the
"Ape-dust" from which the great human spirits of the first
poem have arisen. Read in immediate sequence, as the
poet arranged them, it is made evident to the reader that
the second poem comments on the first; without it "His
Blood" is less of a poem. And, if this is true, the first poem
is also something less than independent: its forward-cast
shadows bring it into a larger unity, from which context it
cannot be completely independent.

"Praise We Great Men" has a reciprocal relationship
not only with "His Blood," but also (as we may now be
prepared to expect), with previous work of the poet. In

particular, it is in "Green Song" that a reader finds adumbration of this poem. By using the line

Return to the hearts of men, those households of high heaven

of "Green Song" as

To the hearts of men, those households of high heaven

the earlier poem, to the close reader, becomes incorporated through its shadow in "Praise We Great Men." Under this consideration the latter poem's

> *Praise be to those who sing*
> *Green hymns of the great waters . . .*

is a kind of eulogy of the poet of "Green Song" which ends its hymneal praise of greenness with reference to "the spirit moving upon the waters." And the older poem's

> *Are we not all of the same substance,*
> *. . . born from the heart of darkness,*
> *Returning to darkness*

is not unlike the passage from "Great Men,"

> *from the first hour*
> *Of the spirit's birth until our earthly setting*
> *Into the night of Death.*

Given the "shadow" of the almost exactly reproduced line and the other similarities between the poems it can be reasonably assumed that some considerable deliberate rapport exists between the two poems. If so, the presence of "Green Song," as that of "His Blood," qualifies and resonates with the poem "Praise We Great Men." The result is to add the more explicit articulation of natural growth, the metaphoric analogies of Spring and greenness, the instructive cycles of death and birth inherent in the seasonal mutations and metamorphoses to the later poem which is primarily descriptive of man's attributes.

Since the poems in this analysis indeed appear to be connected and, in the poet's own phrase, be a part of "collected work," one is persuaded to describe the three poems discussed above as a long hymn on growth with each "independent" poem acting as a part emphasizing a different aspect: "Green Song," the natural; "Praise We Great Men," the human; and "His Blood Colours My Cheek," the divine. But this is not to describe exactly the peculiar relationship among Sitwell's poems that I am attempting to explicate. There is too much autonomy in each of her poems to allow this definition. What is unique about her method of "collecting" and unifying is that she can preserve both the unique and related qualities of each poem.

This duality of the nature of her poetry is another manifestation, perhaps, of her necessity for contrasts. In fact, the especial feature of her "shadowing"—exactitude of repetition—suggests that its purpose is precisely not to violate the integrity or autonomy of the source poem. The quotation is brought as intact as possible to the related poem, varied, perhaps, only to adapt it to the "texture," or stylistic autonomy, of the new context. It is then the reader's work to use that deliberately placed quotation to bring the quoted poem's whole and autonomous meaning to the new poem. Of course, the quoted poem to which we have here attributed "autonomy" may have (and usually does have) analogous "shadows" which in turn relate it to other poems. "Autonomy" is thus relative within Sitwell's canon, as it must be within any organic situation. Nonetheless, there is a large measure of it and the coexistence of this autonomy in a kind of tension with a contrasting dependence is an important aspect of her poetry.

Concerning the forces of unity and independence controlled by her "shadows" Sitwell in *Aspects of Modern Poetry* has quoted a statement of Ezra Pound's which appears to be of significance in explaining her curious repetition (p. 187).

One technical aim of the more accomplished of the modernist poets is to reconcile this necessity of exploring the possibilities of the atom with the necessity for logical design and form.

That Edith Sitwell recognizes the demands of autonomy for the atom—or the single poem—we well know, but that she is concerned with a "collected" work and the disposition of her poems to each other is also a fact. The process here called "shadowing" may be her way of reconciling both demands, those insistent necessities of any organism for both individuation and dependence. (It is also suggestive to compare this poetic technique with her personal and critical temperament so marked with contrasting dispositions to conspicuous self-assertion and the esthetically ordered.) This tension between opposing drives may indeed be manifested in her insistence on a union of whole poems—allusively through a representative "shadow"—into a larger unity in which relative autonomies are still preserved.

Thus, considering these three poems ("Green Song," "Praise We Great Men," and "His Blood Colours My Cheek") as we have, it is something less than correct to say that they constitute a three-part poem. In such a situation there would be embodied a sequential logic and order that is not precisely what we find in Sitwell's process. There is, paradoxically, both more independence and more mutual involvement in Sitwell's ordonnance. For, in any one of these poems the other two are partly embodied and indeed, in a full reading, are to be realized simultaneously with the one under immediate scrutiny; that is, once they have been read, the reader perceives that the poet has altered and qualified the individual autonomies. Each work under this technique becomes larger than itself rather than one-third of a whole. This effect resembles the "rhythmic" relation that E. M. Forster experiences in music and seeks to locate and define in literature. Various movements "all enter the mind at once," he believes, "and extend one another into a common enity." [17] One might also recall Proust's compelling conclusion to *Le Temps retrouvé* in which he declares that men become *géants* when in their imagination "ils touchent simultanément" both the past and the present. It is this sort of enlarging simultaneity that Gertrude Stein remarks in her poem in praise of Edith Sitwell.

She could be as she sleeps and as she walks all day.
                                    She could
be as she sleeps and as she wakes all day is it not so.
It leads it off of that.
Please carried at.
Twice at once and carry.[18]

Miss Stein's insight into Edith Sitwell's peculiar organization as that of "Twice at once and carry" brilliantly epitomizes the work of this chapter in explicating paradigms of that order. And it is this attention of Edith Sitwell's to the connective possibilities (perhaps necessities) amongst the multiple and contrasting—a concern manifest in her criticism as well as in her poetry—that introduces and supports the explicative work of the next chapters: that the imagery of "shadow" becomes, especially in the presence of the images of darkness and light, an important symbol in and of her poetry.

5 THE "DOMINIONS" OF "DARKENESSE AND LIGHT"

EDITH SITWELL has written of Chaucer that he was "a poet of light" who "knew nothing of the black powers that rule the world or the dark places of the heart. It was to the sweet things of the earth, and the 'blissful light,' to an earthly God of growing things, that the gentle giant knelt, 'with dredful hart and glad devocioun.'" [1] Regardless of how accurate an assessment of Chaucer this estimate may be, its tone clearly reveals that to Dame Edith the limited or single vision's ignorance of "the black powers" and "dark places" is no minor qualification of Chaucer's art.

Sitwell's contrasting appreciation of Dylan Thomas is instructive. "In that great poem 'A Refusal to Mourn,'" she remarks, "with its dark, magnificent, proud movement, we see Death in it reality—as a return to the beginning of things, as a robing, a sacred investiture in those who have been our friends since the beginning of Time." [2] In this view the critic of 1920 who praised the "complete and rounded" world of the Diaghilev Ballet which portrayed both "the intense vitality of the heart of life" [3] as well as "the rigidity of death" is also the commentator of 1958: there are in Sitwell's criticism no "early" or "late" divisions. Both "beast and flower," she emphasizes in her approbation of Dylan Thomas, "have their part in the making of mankind. The water drop is holy, the wheat ear is a place of prayer. The 'fathering and all-humbling darkness' itself is a begetting force." [4]

A poet who sought a "vital language—each word possessing an infinite power of germination," Sitwell in her own work also recognizes the real and metaphoric power of both "beast and flower," darkness and light, in the "making of mankind." Her view of the essential unity in a world of contrasts, in particular of light and dark, is characterized by a passage of Sir Thomas Browne's in which he states that "Darkenesse and Light hold interchangeable dominions, and alternately rule the seminal state of things," a passage that Sitwell has included in two of her anthologies.[5]

Despite the implication of her remarks on Chaucer and the emphasis of her appreciation of Dylan Thomas, Edith Sitwell does employ the imagery of light—and especially the sun—and its seminal relationship to life more frequently than the imagery of darkness. It is, apparently, this very emphasis of the poet herself which in part may account for the general impression that her poetry is of a "garden world."[6] Certainly this impression is confirmed by the very titles of a large number of her works: *Bucolic Comedies, Green Song, Gardeners and Astronomers, A Book of Flowers, Look, The Sun!, The Canticle of the Rose, Rustic Elegies*, and *Troy Park*. L. P. Hartley observes of Edith Sitwell "that again and again she returns to the positive, life-giving symbols of the Sun, the Lion and the Rose."[7] And C. M. Bowra demonstrates that "Sitwell shows how the whole natural and human scene is transformed by the power of light,"[8] an observation supported by these lines from her "Holiday."

> *Beneath the flowering boughs of heaven*
> *The country roads are made of thickest gold;*
> *They stretch beyond the world, and light like snow*
> *Falls where we go, the Intelligible Light*
> *Turns all to gold, the apple, the dust, the unripe wheat ear.*

In the early poetry what is most frequently remarked by critics is the scenery "bright as a seedsman's packet"[9] where "skies shone like the fields . . . Golden with buttercups and dew."[10]

In the later work critics consistently emphasize the humane harvest where a benevolent

> sun is the first lover of the world
> Blessing all humble creatures, all life-giving,
> Blessing the end of life and the work done,
> The clean and the unclean, ones in earth and splendors
> Within the heart of man, that second sun.[11]

Sitwell's apostrophe,

> O bright gold of the heat of the Sun
> Of Love across dark fields—burning away rough husks of
>   Death
> Till all is fire, and bring all to Harvest! [12]

has not gone unnoticed or unheeded. Bowra, for example, writes in 1948 of Sitwell's vision that "whatever wounds mankind may inflict upon itself, whatever it may suffer from decay and destitution, it can in the end be healed by finding itself in harmony with the powers of nature and with the light and the love that informs them." [13] Subsequent scholarship continues to emphasize Sitwell's imagery of sun.[14] "Golden," Grigson declares in 1965, is "Miss Sitwell's key word." [15]

This criticism that concentrates on Sitwell's garden world of sun and love is perhaps best illustrated by John Piper's comment that "Once, as a girl—perhaps a very little girl—inside a garden, Edith Sitwell's senses must have had a sudden blow, enduring in its effect." According to Piper she is thereafter continuously concerned with that moment in which

> she sees sunshot walls of brick and rich-textured stone, scarlet flowers, golden fruit, perhaps hears a voice drifting from the lake, through the warm yellow air, or a movement or a sound of music: the moment has become for her the measure of all poetry and all passion for ever.[16]

The question which Sitwell herself asks in "Harvest,"

> For is not the blood—the divine, the animal heat
> That is not fire—derived from the solar ray?

seems to be unequivocally answered. Yet the poet herself in the same poem speaks of

> The laughing heat of the Sun that was born from darkness—
> Returning to darkness.

Fulfilling the definition of Sir Thomas Browne, that the dominion of "darkenesse" can be interchanged as a seminal state with that of light, Sitwell repeats the theme in "Green Song."

Are we not all of the same substance
Man, planets, and earth, born from the heart of darkness
Returning to darkness.

The fuller reading of Edith Sitwell's poetry discovers in the midst of her "green rejoicing" and "the golden stalk of the young long-petalled flower of the sun" (from "Green Song") her more comprehensive conceit. If in "How Many Heavens" the primacy of light is "established,"

The yellow straws of light,
Whereof the sun has built his nest, cry "Bright
Is the world, the yellow straw
My brother—God is the straw within the straw:—All things
  are Light,"

the reader must also be disposed to accommodate, in the same poem, the metaphysical reversal,

> *He is the green shade that came*
> *To be the heart of shade.*

And in the same collection (*Street Songs*) the poet affirms in "Song" ("We are the darkness") that

> *We are the darkness in the heat of the day*
>   *. . . Beauty's daughter,*
> *The heart of the rose, and we are one*
>   . . . .
> *That sun and its false light scorning.*

This dominion of darkness, although less prominent in Sitwell's work than that of light, is interesting and important to the critic of Sitwell, because without it—as she indicates consistently throughout her criticism—the poet is incomplete. She praises Yeats, for example, because not only does he possess the "radiance of eternity" but also "the wisdom that lies hidden in the heart of darkness." Moreover, the generating force which she frequently grants to darkness is more compelling than that of light, and despite her frequent compliance with Browne's view of interchangeable seminal states she ultimately credits darkness with the original state. In repeating that the "Sun" and "men, planets, and earth" are "born from the heart of darkness" she affirms the teaching of Genesis, "In the beginning . . . darkness was . . . And God said let there be light." In asking "Does not each dark root hold a world of Gold?" (in "Gardeners and Astronomers") she clearly allies herself with a tradition of metaphysical poetry which she has extensively cited in her criticism and included in her anthologies.

She prints in *A Book of the Winter* the passage from a sermon of John Donne's, "He brought light out of darkness, not out of a lesser light." Cowley's "Hymn, To Light," which opens with

> *First born of Chaos, who so fair didst come*
> *From the old Negro's darksome womb*

is in her *British and American Poetry* as is Crashaw's "Hymn of the Nativity" with its classic conceit,

> *Wellcome, all wonders in one sight!*
> *Aeternity shut in a span.*
> *Summer in Winter, Day in Night,*

which in one sense presents Summer and Day as contained in, and therefore less than Winter and Night.

But her metaphysical conception of darkness may be best characterized by her interest in Lord Herbert of Cherbury's "Sonnet of Black Beauty."

> *Black beauty, which above that common light,*
>   *Whose Power can no colours here renew,*
>   *But those which darkness can again subdue,*
> *Do'st still remain unvary'd to the sight,*
>
> *And like an object equal to the view,*
>   *Art neither chang'd with day, nor hid with night:*
>   *When all these colours which the world call bright,*
> *And which old Poetry doth so persue,*
>
> *Are with the night so perished and gone,*
>   *That of their being there remains no mark,*

> *Thou still abidest so intirely one,*
>   *That we may know thy blackness is a spark*
> *Of light inaccessible, and alone*
>   *Our darkness which can make us think it dark.*

Mentioning on a BBC television interview that the Sitwells were descended from the Herberts, she called Lord Herbert a "remarkable poet," an opinion confirmed by the inclusion of this poem in both her *Book of the Winter* and *Atlantic Book of British and American Poetry*. For Lord Herbert in "Black Beauty" it is "old Poetry" that "doth so persue" the "colours which the world call bright." Presumably to him it is a new poetry—Sitwell's no less than Herbert's—which partakes of and sponsors the conceited metamorphosis from Darkness to Light. "The miracle of poetry," Edith Sitwell stated early in her career, is its "birth of jangling water from the darkest earth." [17]

In regard to this conception of the birth of light and life from darkness it is significant that whereas Dylan Thomas speaks of the "fathering" darkness, a view to which Edith Sitwell indeed assents, she in addition describes darkness as a maternal force, a concept that may be said to emphasize even more the relevance of darkness to birth. The Dark is not just "seminal" or "begetting," but the actual matrix or embodiment of life. "Darkness" in "Green Song" is significantly "the consoling mother." And these lines,

Men, planets, and earth, born from the heart of darkness
Returning to darkness, the consoling mother

give further insight into the importance of her first poetry collected as *The Mother*. When the speaker of one of her later poems says "My birth was Darkness," [18] the state of Edith Sitwell's own poetry in those early "dark" pieces is accurately described.

Darkness as a begetting and consoling image pervades the five poems of *The Mother*: the three brief pieces, "Drowned Suns," "The Web of Eros," "Serenade"; and the longer poems, "The Drunkard" and "The Mother."

In previous chapters the references to "Drowned Suns," her first published poem, indicated that darkness, or half-darkness, was the realm in which "lost suns" are sought. The augury or seed of hope in that beginning was seen to be effectively emphasized by her last poem "Music and Ceremonies" which in its affirmation of fulfillment recollected that "the beginning" which "leads to the end" is not idyllic: "the lilies' growth arises/From all the weight of earth, the centuries," and "dark are music's springs."

In "The Web of Eros," the second poem of the collection, the theme of love as entanglement is appropriately evoked by the interaction of the contrasting images of Sitwell's poetic vision. "The evening air" turns to "gold" when "the stars of heaven sang for joy." "The cold earth" feels the "maenad fire of spirng," and the "myrrh-lit flame brings both death and birth to the soul Phoenix." The use of the image of the Phoenix is noteworthy because the image is almost never used again in her poetry, although its symbolism of metamorphosis—of death begetting life, the conciliation of opposites—is apparently her abiding theme. And it is pertinent here to suggest a reason for its neglect after "The Web of Eros."

This poem is obviously apprentice work; the author herself did not include it in any subsequent edition of collected poems. The banality of the imagery of "gold," "stars," "spring" to describe love is obvious; the only interest the poem has is in its paradigm of opposition and irony which will be fulfilled with more compelling originality in other and later poems. The image of the Phoenix, moreover, does not really encompass enough ironic opposition to manifest Sitwell's "necessity of contrast." The restoration of the Phoenix—its return to light, so to speak—is accomplished by fire, which image, of course, is also of light and brightness. For the fullest embodiment of the genetic conceit of birth out of death she will need an image and symbol more closely associated, not only with light but even more meaningfully with darkness.

The importance of "Serenade," the third poem of *The*

Mother, may be confirmed by its initial position in Sitwell's *Collected Poems* (the preceding two poems of *The Mother* are not included). Literally a night-piece, the poem established the primacy and fertility of darkness. The opening lines,

> *The tremulous gold of stars within your hair*
> *Are yellow bees flown from the hive of night*

introduce us to a world of contrast and irony held in meaningful accord. The sun's color is attributed to the night's stars, perhaps because the poet already perceives a causative relationship between darkness and light, night and day. In the second line the "yellow bees" are born from the mothering "hive" of night. The darkness of the evening world must be experienced, the poet requests,

> *Then, Sweet, awake, and ope your dreaming eyes*
> *Ere those bright bees have flown and darkness dies.*

It is, apparently, only out of and against the "darkness" that such "bright" beauty can be seized. The concluding line may mean either that when the brightness ("bright bees") ceases then darkness also dies or that when "darkness dies" what it has begot also dies. But in either case—and the ambiguity may be informing—her earliest poetry confirms the interdependence as well as the necessity of contrasts, the unity within diversity that she has spoken of so often in her own criticism of poetry.

Yet, in these first three short poems of *The Mother,* the dominant tone is so romantic and sentimental that a modern taste is repelled: it is again perhaps, only the thesis of the generative power of darkness that attracts a contemporary reader. It is only in "The Drunkard," the fourth poem of this collection, that Sitwell begins to emerge as a poet with a modern style, in this instance, a style calculated to disturb the expectations of early Georgian readers. The opening lines of "The Drunkard" are its most effective ones perhaps because they most strikingly employ the contrast of black and white.

> This black tower drinks the blinding light,
> Strange windows livid white,
>
> Tremble beneath the curse of God.

The subsequent three lines continue the technique of bold and ironic contrast,

> Yet living weeds still nod
>
> To the huge sun, a devil's eye
> That tracks the souls that die.

Here blackness "drinks" light, and apparently is made blacker by the "blinding" light; life must look for sustenance in a sun which is a "devil's eye" that times and covets death. "Darkenesse and Light," from the outset of Sitwell's work, can also beget horror.

"The Mother," the longest and the most ambitious poem of the first collection, at the beginning of her career most explicitly establishes her later statement that "darkness" can be a "consoling mother" and a "begetting" force. The speaker of the poem recounts her murder by her son whose wife

> came
> False-hearted as Hell's blackest shame
> To steal my child

and of whom we read that

> Her eyes were black as Hell's own night,
> Her ice-cold breast was winter-white.

The *extreme* intensities of blackness and whiteness attributed to the wife readily convey, in terms that are understandably Sitwell's, the mother's revulsion toward her. Yet the poem is not a study of a mother's insane jealousy, although that possibility through much of the work adds to the poem's complexity and power. The mother does not shrilly denounce the daughter-in-law to the end, but finally blames her own son as her murderer, and, in a moving collocation which obtains its force from a bitter irony of situation, longs to comfort him,

> *I cannot draw his head to rest*
> *Deep down upon my wounded breast . . .*
> *He gave the breast that fed him well*
> *To suckle the small worms of Hell.*

The mother's agony brings vision; the mother finally indicts neither son nor wife, but herself,

> *He did not sin. But cold blind earth*
> *The body was that gave him birth.*
> *All mine, all mine the sin; the love*
> *I bore him was not deep enough.*

Out of the anguish of the grave where she heard her

> *pierced heart scream*
> *His name within the dark*

comes at last the birth of "cold blind" jealousy's opposite: humble repentance and full forgiveness.

Remembering that Edith Sitwell came to praise the Russian (Diaghilev) Ballet for its "complete and rounded" world, and Dylan Thomas for holding within his poetic vision both "beast and flower," it is understandable that these early pieces of *The Mother* would not for long be satisfactory to their author. The first three lyrics — "Drowned Suns," "The Web of Eros," and "Serenade" — are in tone all "flower," while the macabre "The Drunkard" and the hell-harrowing "The Mother" are so unrelieved in terror as to be almost melodramatic. The continuing process of her work supports the hypothesis that her important endeavor is to achieve, in Crashaw's terms, the blending of "both the noons of night and day." [19] The reconciliation — in tone and imagery as well as theme — of warring opposites appears to be the main course of her poetry.

Her next published collection, *Twentieth-Century Harlequinade* (a joint work with her brother Osbert) of 1916 alludes in its very title to the clashing contrasts of her era. Her "Pedagogues" from this volume vividly manifests the strife and opposition,

> *The air is like a jarring bell*
> *That jangles words it cannot spell.*

In this setting the "iron trees" are "black as Fate," the "hot sun" has a "patronizing stare," the "noisy light" is "parrot-bright." The "sheen of sands" shines "beneath the giddy lights of noon." Yet there is an attempt at and a possibility of crude understanding in this desert where "iron trees/Stretch thirstily to catch the breeze."

The "snorting" of "the brass band" (presumably of pedagogues)

> *stabs the sky*
> *And tears the yielding vacancy—*
> *The imbecile and smiling blue—*
> *Until fresh meaning trickles through.*

The fifth and sixth stanzas at this point of the poem then define explicitly the "curse" of the age, and in particular, the folly of "we"—poets, therefore, included as "pedagogues"—who would teach and direct. Not only do poets ("we") write as if for children, "And slowly we perambulate," but, perhaps, because of that, their vision is limited

> *With spectacles that concentrate*
> *In one short hour, Eternity,*
> *In one small lens, Infinity.*

This foreshortened and puerile view predominates because "we" concern ourselves

> *With children, our primeval curse,*

and because of this "child-centered" perspective

> *We overrun the universe.*

"Overrun" suggests here not mere physical creation, but more significantly the distorting neglect of the complexities of reality by a simplistic and narrow concern.

"Our primeval curse," according to "Pedagogues," is not in begetting, for that theme would be a perversion of Sitwell's dedication to the seminal and vital. The "curse" here is in preventing growth, in reducing all—"Eternity" and "Infinity"—by "one small lens" to the childish. Existence in such a world remains primary and jejune. The poem concludes as it began with life reduced and shrunken, with the air like

> *a jarring bell*
> *That jangles words it cannot spell,*
> *And, black as Fate, the iron trees*
> *Stretch thirstily to catch the breeze.*

The poem incisively demonstrates how much Edith Sitwell detested that which prevents the growth of poetry. Although this theme is especially prominent in the era of *Wheels* (and "Pedagogues"), she never abandoned this battle for art: the dedication of her last book (1965), recalling the intrusion upon Coleridge that curtailed "Kubla Khan," is to "The Persons from Porlock." The book is primarily an indictment of those who had "overrun" or "taken care of" her.

Appearing in June 1916 just before she published her first issue of *Wheels* in December of that year, "Pedagogues" elucidates much of the poet's developing attitude and tone about poetic comprehension of a "rounded universe" or "beast and flower," of "Darkenesse" as well as "Light." The author has chosen only this poem from *Twentieth-Century Harlequinade* for inclusion in her "collected work."

The shocked reactions to the first cycle of *Wheels* may reveal how little understood was Edith Sitwell's earlier work which indeed seems to explain or "introduce" the venture of *Wheels*. Of course, Sitwell set out to elicit that provoked response, but more than a gadfly—although a very effective one—she appears to have used exasperated ignorance as part of her dramatization of the need for a new and more meaningful integrity and comprehension in poetry.

Many of the derogatory responses to *Wheels* have a common theme: "The foetidness of the whole clings to the nostrils," [20] "The ability is uncurbed in its choice of subject, and its imagination is unwholesome," [21] "a most sad and dismal view of this dim spot which men call earth." [22] Such opinions suggest that the commentators had little understood the theme of *The Mother* where "foetidness" is not solely disgusting but already embodies something of Sitwell's later interpretation (of "Gardeners and Astronomers") in which

> gardeners
> *See all miasmas from the human filth but as the dung*
> *In which to sow great flowers,*
> *Tall moons and mornings, seeds, and sires and suns.*

An understanding of that important poem "Pedagogues" might have made clearer that the new poetry must not betray the truths of reality with a childish exclusion of all that does not please. In brief, what appears to have been misunderstood about the poetry of *Wheels* was its editor's view that poetry as a living and growing organism experiences both sunshine and darkness, and does, in fact, in the very cyclical nature of life grow in the presence of and even out of darkness, decay and death.

It is this organic and viable conception of poetry that apparently informs the *épatant* cover of the first cycle of *Wheels:* an amateurish line drawing of a nursemaid pushing a perambulator. Against the bright yellow background of the cover Sitwell's friend Phylis Boyd has also drawn a parasol to shade an infant from the sun that dominates the horizon. Yet there has been no satisfactory explication of this drawing, the shocking strangeness of which seems to make it an integral part of Edith Sitwell's manifesto and the spirit of *Wheels.* The *New Statesman,* at publication, said, "It is rather stupid to put a picture of a nursemaid wheeling a perambulator with a baby in it on the cover. None of the contributors can be quite so young as that." [23] A recent critic suggests that "the illustration symbolizes the general youthfulness of the poets whose works are published within." [24]

Ezra Pound, in his review of *Wheels* in *Poetry,* had a more interesting speculation about the significance of the cover which he saw as "pleasingly satiric . . . the proper sort of ink-pot to hurl itself into the face of senile pomposity." [25] But Pound continues to state that

Here, however, the gaiety ends and the contents of the book have none of the lightness of Miss Sitwell's earlier couplet:

> *With children our primeval curse*
> *We overrun the universe.*

In this statement Pound appears to be incontestably and inexplicably wrong. How could he call "Pedagogues" (from which "the earlier couplet" comes) a gay and light poem? If "gaiety" is to be found there, the more exact description of it is to be found in Edith Sitwell's own phrase which she applied to Laforgue—"terrible gaiety."

In "Antic Hay," of *Wheels* 1916, the "lightness" and "gaiety" of the couplet

> *Beneath dark chestnut trees, King Pan doth sport*
> *With all his horned court,*

well represents the special kind of metric and thematic "sport" to be found in both "Pedagogues" and Sitwell's subsequent poetry including her work in *Wheels*. One can understand why Edith Sitwell in reprinting Pound's statement in her "Press Notices" of *Wheels* appended her note about "stupidity."

Pound is right, however, in detecting satire in the 1916 cover, and he is also perceptive in sensing the relevance of "Pedagogues" to the cartoon. Still the insistent question is, if in "Pedagogues" (June 1916) Sitwell derides poets who "slowly . . . perambulate" and "overrun the universe" (i.e., reduce all to infantile simplicity) what does the perambulator embody on the cover of *Wheels* (December 1916)? It would be reasonable to assume some relevance between the two occasions, but it could hardly be that the cover signifies the simplistic outlook of the poets within, that they too are perambulating pedagogues. The relationship between the conception of "pedagogues" and the cover of *Wheels* appears to be that the poets of *Wheels* are obliquely characterized by the outrageously simple depiction of what they are *not*. The power of such an ironic approach is that by emphasizing the object ("nanny" narrowness) of the volume's satire the poems within are twice described: by that simplistic distortion which they do not possess and which they seek to counteract. Moreover, the ironic technique itself supports the thesis of complexity which *Wheels* manifests.

Contrary to Pound's implication the cover seems to be very much the accurate projection of the contents: the poetry that follows also satirizes the pervading and excluding world of the nursemaid's guardian outlook. This position is supported by Sitwell's later introduction to the *Atlantic Book of British and American Poetry* in which she decries "much of the poetry from 1880 to 1915" as written for the "Man in the Street, to provide simple vehicles for his simple thoughts and scratchy cotton gloves to protect his hands from the truth of reality." In this denunciation of "minor versifiers" she notes that

> There is now a general clamoring for the use of the Vulgar Tongue, "to which," said Dante (who would, I fear, be disdained were he of our day), "infants, when they first begin to distinguish sounds, are accustomed by those about them. Or still more shortly, we call that the Vulgar Tongue which, without any rules at all, we get by imitating our nurses." (*De Vulgaris Eloquio*).

Then, in keeping with the satiric rejection of the nursemaid world by the *Wheels* 1916 cover, she adds, "But in most cases poetry should, to quote a phrase of Ben Jonson, 'speak above a mortal mouth'" (p. xiii).

The cover may even have a third relevance to the enclosed poetry, since by suggesting (and rejecting) one kind of pedagogic blindness or myopia it may also be representative of a new vision, a new pedagogy. In this dimension, therefore, the cover drawing may also be seen as directly representing the new perambulation in which the nursemaid may be the enlightened poet (not necessarily young) and the infant the new poetry which under a far seeing wisdom shall indeed be allowed to grow to maturity, to "speak above a mortal mouth."

These symbolic and allusive interpretations are supported not only by the poem "Pedagogues," but also by the bright yellow color of the cover. For in some respects

Wheels seems to have appeared as a new *Yellow Book* with much of the allusive suggestion of that publication and even the color itself of which Katharine Lyon Mix gives the following summary.

> Yellow had assumed significance before the dawn of 1890. A favorite color with the Pre-Raphaelites, with Rossetti and Burne-Jones, it was also affected by Whistler. . . .
>
> Yellow sunflowers, painted on the walls of the Oxford Union by William Morris, became the symbol of aestheticism in the hand of Oscar Wilde, who praised the leonine, gaudy beauty of the flower so fervently that American undergraduates at Harvard and Yale marched to his lectures bearing stalks of the yellow blossoms.[26]

Of especial interest is the remark of the editor of *Harper's* whose statement on "Yellow Literature" very much resembles many of the opinions on *Wheels*. "The Yellow literature is not new," he said, adding, "There have always been diseased people seeking notoriety by reason of their maladies." Of the *Yellow Book* Miss Mix observes in her *Study in Yellow* (p. 3) that

> It was undoubtedly the Yellow Book that gave to the color its final importance. Published at the Bodley Head by John Lane with Henry Harland and Aubrey Beardsley as editors, bound like a book in strong durable cloth, the periodical began in April, 1894, and ended in April, 1897. Those thirteen fat volumes in their staring black and yellow covers took their place on library shelves as a symbol of the period, documentary evidence for posterity.

The simple line drawing on the cover of the first cycle of *Wheels* is conceivably Edith Sitwell's latter-day counterpart of Aubrey Beardsley's drawing on the initial cover of the *Yellow Book*. Although Beardsley's "plump masked woman . . . smiling encouragingly at the approach of her swain"—as described by Mix (p. 87)—evokes a sexual theme, as indeed Phylis Boyd's nanny and infant do not, both covers sought to outrage an oppressively artificial society. And in that related role both drawings and publications succeeded in irritating a considerable public.

Moreover, despite an absolute absence in Sitwell's work of even a suspicion of eroticism, there are some remarkable affinities of her with Beardsley. For example, his illustrations for the "Rape of the Lock" reveal an interest in Pope; his use of a monkey as a symbol of decadence (as in his "Woman with a Monkey") is paralleled throughout her early poetry; and his depiction of the *Commedia del arte* figures, *Il Dottore*, *Arlecchino*, and *Pierrot* (as in "The Death of Pierot") calls to mind her own extensive presentation of those characters. Her footnote to her poem "Black Coffee" (*Clown's Houses*, 1918) states that it "was derived from a drawing by Aubrey Beardsley."

The second appearance of *Wheels*—the reissue of the first volume with added press notices—demonstrated visibly that if *Wheels* did utilize in its role some recollection of yellow, yellow literature and the *Yellow Book*, it was to be no exact imitation of the *Yellow Book*. The complete cover of this second issue was a flat black that almost obscured the slightly darker lines of the nursemaid and pram. The birth of *Wheels* is celebrated in light and darkness.

These "twin" issues of *Wheels* in 1916, the first in yellow, the second in black, are an informing manifestation of the very real necessity of contrast and in particular of the imagery of darkness and light that pervades Edith Sitwell's work from its beginnings. In the first issue of *Wheels*, for example, we find the realms of night and day, of Moon and Sun appreciated individually and jointly. Each element contributes to her world, as indicated in these juxtaposed lines,

> *The Moon did give me silver pence,*
> *The Sun did give me gold*

from "The King of China's Daughter." More importantly, when these forces combine "And both together softly blew"—in a synaesthetic distortion that stresses intermixture—then fulfillment is effected. But love's harmony is denied when, in contrast to the consonance of the Sun and Moon, "the King of China's daughter"

> *Pretended not to see*
> *When I hung my cap and bells upon*
> *Her nutmeg tree.*

As implied in her observations of Chaucer and Dylan
Thomas (and in all of her critical comment) there can be
no evasion of realities: only loss and diminution attend
the abridged view, the view that, in the sense of "Pedagogues," "overruns the universe." Three decades later in
"Heart and Mind" she still emphasizes the reconciliation
of opposites in terms analogous to those of "The King of
China's Daughter." "We shall mate no more," the Lion
of the late poem says to the Lioness, "Till the fire of that
Sun the heart and the moon-cold bone are one."

This necessity for synthesis is most effectively presented
in a poem from *Wheels* of 1918. Through the striking
metaphor of the piano keyboard she cogently manifests in
"The Avenue" how the "dominions" of "darkenesse and
light" unresolved by connective conceit or harmony are
inadequate to sustain or represent the generative complexity—for Sitwell, the excellence—of human life.

The setting for "The Avenue," a "huge and glassy
room," appears to be her "Hell," a scene confirmed by her
poem of the next year, "Mandoline." In this later work
the monkey Fanfreluche who also appears in "The Avenue" "scratches" his mandoline in "the huge house of
glass" definitively placed, "Down in Hell's gilded street."
But even without the clarifying relevance of the other
poem, "The Avenue"—in describing the primal and bestial world out of which evolving life ascends—clearly suggests a kind of low or hellish world. It is significant that in
these two poems Sitwell establishes as hell that which
man in his "growth of consciousness" works out of.

"The Avenue" opens as Pantaloon the parrot watches
Fanfreluche

> *Fawn upon the piano keys*
> *Flatter till they answer back,*
> *Through the scale of centuries,*
> *Difference between white and black.*

Significantly the verbs "fawn" and "flatter" here in context are not entirely of pejorative value, because they effect an "answer" and are a step, albeit a beginning one, in Sitwell's depiction of the evolution of meaning. These ape-like attempts are the beginnings of relationship and connection.

In explicating Edith Sitwell's emphasis on correlation, thematically and formally, it may be useful to allude briefly to another modern poet who offers a contrasting theme. In the poetry of Robert Frost one finds little, if any "answering back." Frost asks "questions that have no reply," and seeks to honor and enlarge in his poetry "the diminished thing" [27] of isolation. The fragile flight of the butterfly in "The Tuft of Flowers," the attempted flight *toward* the distant mower and then its tremulous return *almost* to the speaker of the poem, brilliantly expresses the nature of real or substantive connection between men in Frost's poetry. When he does achieve, in this poem, an imaginative communion with the unseen mower,

> *a spirit kindred to my own*
> *So that henceforth I worked no more alone,*

the ending of the poem,

> *'Men work together,' I told him from the heart,*
> *Whether they work together or apart,*

with its final emphasis on "apart" (he had begun the poem with "I") serves to establish as the dominant force of the poem the justification of isolation. [28]

Similarly, in "Mending Wall" the speaker does not categorically object to separation or a wall: he would only wish that each builder or mender have his own, not his father's, reason for the barrier. He would prefer that his opposite number "say it for himself." Also "speaking of contraries," Frost's poem "West-running Brook" cogently presents the poet's abiding theme of a multiverse of confirmed diversity. Significantly, the man and wife—the speakers of the poem—ask "What are we?" And their answer emphasizes the elements rather than the unity of their marriage,

> 'We must be something
> We've said we two.'

Moreover, they seek to add to the multiplicity of their worlds,

> Let's change that to we three.
> As you and I are married to each other,
> We'll both be married to the brook.

The poem depicts, in terms of the brook, the movement

> Against the stream, that most we see ourselves in,

and there is no apparent change of the individual within the new role of a union. The poem ends as the speakers concur in granting autonomy to each other:

> 'Today will be the day
> You said so.'

> 'No. Today will be the day
> You said the brook was called West-running Brook.'

> 'Today will be the day of what we both said.'

The resulting combination is a mixture which does not change the individual elements, except to strengthen or enable their individuality. Frost's conceits are not of tempering, reconciliation or synthesis: he celebrates individual theses and antitheses. The love that evolves in a poem like Sitwell's "The Mother" (and which will be a dominant theme throughout her work) is of marked contrast to the autonomous selfhood sponsored by the poetry of Frost.

The "scale of centuries"—the organism's struggle for improvement in "The Avenue"—involves for Sitwell the individuation between the keys, and in this part of her conceit she, like Frost, asserts the individual. But the contrasting colors and meanings are simultaneously perceived and held in the harmony of a single keyboard, the temperament and balance that is implied in "scale."

The work of comprehending the individual complexities of the keyboard's unity changes the keyboard from the singleness of "the blackest vacuums" to the complexity of a "light-barred avenue," clearly the way to meaning and fulfillment of man's and life's generative possibilities.

When the "semi-tones," that is, the harmonic relationship between black and white, are discovered—but within the overriding unity—

> *Then, from matter, life comes.*

Although the lines principally describe the "Bestial efforts at man's soul," the poem emerges as Sitwell's definition of the process of "soul-making," from which

> *Soon the shapeless tune comes*

and

> *Meaning comes to bind the whole.*

"The Avenue," however, concludes with these disturbing lines,

> *Fundamentally*
> *I am you, and you are me—*
> *Octaves fall as emptily*

which epitomize a primal undifferentiated condition—"the shapeless tune," the "blackest vacuums." But why does the poet, after describing the sequence of soul-shaping from the stumbling on keys to the perception of meaning, return again to the beginning of the cycle? Is this reversal a pessimistic augury? The evidence of the poem suggests that it is not. Immediately preceding the three concluding lines (and following the assertion of the emergence of meaning) the poet asks

> *What though notes are false and shrill—*
> *Black streets tumbling down a hill?*

The conclusion then reassuringly emphasizes that only "fundamentally" are things "emptily" alike, an emphasis which suggests the possibilities of progressing from the fundamental to the superior. The last line similarly suggests that if "Octaves fall . . . emptily" other combinations of the keyboard—harmonic ones—compose more satisfying combinations of diversity. Sitwell's "Hell" is transcended by a condition of *das Ewig-Weibliche* and "images that yet fresh images beget."

The concluding reprise of emptiness effectively represents the struggle and failure involved in the attaining of intelligence and meaning. Moreover, this concluding allusion to beginnings is provocatively appropriate to the poem's title. "Avenue" occurs three times in the short work, each usage denoting the progressive quality of the "efforts at man's soul." Sitwell proclaims that "meaning comes to bind the whole," but that is only after the way ("keys," "promenades," "black streets") has been undertaken and traversed. An "avenue" can be an approach, usually to a considerable edifice; this poem asserts a beginning and a direction. The goal—a fulfilled "growth of consciousness," the necessity of which is proclaimed in this "key" poem—will be her "collected work." Since Sitwell, as we have seen in a preceding chapter, described another poet's body of work as his Parthenon, perhaps "The Avenue" may be usefully described as a way or approach to her own realizing structure of art.

But the announcement of "The Avenue" is not at all to be construed as the disappearance of the contrasting dominions of "darkenesse and light" into the blending symbol of "shadow." It is not at all to direct us to an allusive "empire of shade" which shall not further utilize the imagery of the more elemental states of night and day, Sun and Moon, dark and light. These images will not vanish from the poetry of Edith Sitwell—as acknowledged in the earlier statement of the chapter that the Sun is the dominant image in her poetry, "early," "middle," and "late." And if we consider the nature of shadow as a phenomenon we will immediately realize one reason for the continuing presence of the poles of darkness and light even after the full evolution of the richer and more allusive image and symbol "shadow." A shadow cannot exist without the begetting presence of light, in particular the sun. Moreover, its effect of relief and refuge from the sun's desiccating intensity cannot be appreciated except in the actual presence of that begetting sun. In a similar way, the imagery of darkness contributes, through comparison, to a fuller appreciation of "shadow" as image, metaphor and ultimately symbol.

As a shadow cannot exist without sun so is the shadow's symbolism inadequately realized without an understanding of the powers and states which it resolves and unifies. In the "Interlude" from *Gardeners and Astronomers* the agony of the poet derives from "the intolerable weight of tyrant suns" and the "azoic azure," but her "azoic heart" is also manifested in terms of the "azoic continent of night and stone." This use of darkness and light reinforces and informs the lines from "Out of School" of the same collection.

> The shadow of the crooked and the straight
> Complete each other, and the cripple's hump,
> The curve of the mountain hiding veins of gold
> As equal in their grandeur.

It is with such a highly conceited vision of shadow that we "set right the inharmonious errors of our lives" beholding that

The elements are but as qualities
That change for ever, like all things that have known
*   generation, like a gold*
Image taking a new form for ever.

If shadow becomes her symbol of harmonic relationship (as I believe it does) it will be important in part because it coexists with—and tempers—the elementary and "fundamental" states. Among the imagery of "intolerable" extremes it is the embodied proof of generation and viable mutation.

The use of the contrasting extremes of light and dark as "intolerable extremes" to set off the efficacy of the image "shadow" is, however, not the sole use of that imagery. Although the "light-barred" avenue is clearly the approbative metaphor for life in "The Avenue," the polar extremes of light and dark—"Jungles splashed with violent light" and "Black streets tumbling down a hill" are nonetheless not here nor in many instances of the poetry ("early" or "late") presented with absolute revulsion. Writing always with an abiding conception that the fulfilling vision is a comprehensive one, in fact, one evolving from a synthesis of experience both radiant and dark, she frequently treats the single (undifferentiated) aspects with an awareness of their dialectical participation in an evolving resolution.

This perspective accounts in part for the "gaiety" of much of her early work. Pantaloon of "The Avenue" can be "panached . . . with many a plume," and Fanfreluche can be in "gilded ruche" not because they are symbols of honorific or "delectable" values, but because they may represent beginnings of a kind of eventual victory. Sitwell is disposed to appreciate the auspicious, however crude. Behind the "crude-striped wooden face" of "Springing Jack," another of her "early" poems, she tells us that "dust bears seeds that grow to grace." The contrasts created by a universe of process are clearly seen in her Jack which has a

> Clear angel-face on hairy stalk
> (Soul grown from flesh, an ape's young talk).

The puppet is "tinsel-pink" not simply because he frivolously can "leap on . . . springs," but also because in so performing he will "learn how to think." And

> Then, like the trembling stalk
> Of some long-petalled star

he will

> walk
> Through the dark heavens, until dew
> Falls . . . and sense thrills through.

The complexity of Sitwell's vision, even in the "early" poems, is manifest. The irony of her "gaiety," of course, does purposefully evoke a certain "terrible" revulsion as in this description from "Mandoline" where

> Down in Hell's gilded street
> Snow dances fleet and sweet
> Bright as a parakeet,
>
> Or Punchinello,
> All glistening yellow,
> As fruit-jewels mellow,

Glittering white and black
As the swan's glassy back
On the Styx' soundless track.

But here, in addition to the ironic gaiety, the primitive poles of "glittering white" or "glistening yellow" and "black" would posit a kind of "Hell" to Sitwell and explain why "Hell's gilded street" is also an "empty street." Hell, as we have seen, to Sitwell is the static, the undeveloping, the undifferentiated whether bright or dark, white or black. This is why, as with Sir Thomas Browne, a seminal state may be either of "darkenesse" or "light"; a beginning may be made from either realm. Hell to Sitwell is, as in her "Mandoline," that which is "sharp," "shrieking," "stinging bright," of "sharp tang and sheen," "sharp as bird's painted bill." There is no harmony or tempering, no scale, no "whole" to be bound and therefore no meaning. Hell is "empty," and it is this desolation—especially "terrible" and allusive in its brightness—that is so skillfully evoked by many of her early poems.

The exaggerated monotony of "Sir Beelzebub" [29] aptly demonstrates the hellishness of the unrelieved and undifferentiated. In that concluding poem of *Façade* the unchanging "classical metre" of "Alfred Lord Tennyson" leads us to the final anguished cry, "None of them come!" Hell can be fashionable and elegant—and bright; Beelzebub, in Sitwell's conception, can be a British lord demanding bar service in his hotel as long as his habitat is sterile and barren and no thing or person experiences growth or fulfillment. Essentially, Sitwell's conception of hell accords with Dante's portrayal of the Inferno's central frigid immobility. In "Mandoline" "snow dances" in "Hell's gilded street," and significantly, in the midst of "adder flames," "the cold is appalling." Both poets appear to utilize this irony for the rhetorical impact of their hells, although the conception is also theologically valid, since acedia with its paralysis of the will has been traditionally considered the most "deadly" of sins.

"Technically," as I have recalled throughout this study, Edith Sitwell has written, "I would come to a vital language—each word possessing an infinite power of germination." Not only has she demonstrated formally this theory of growth through relationship in her criticism and the organization of her poetry, but, as the exposition of this chapter has attempted to indicate, she also employs her imagery in a highly allusive and germinative manner. One image begets another; the presence of one quality suggests the absence of another or others. The juxtaposition of extremes fathers the image to contain them—as in the piano keyboard of "The Avenue." Her vision, as Yeats remarked, is indeed "double": in *Gold Coast Customs* even the "squealing light" is "striped black and white," and in "Trio for Two Cats and a Trombone" (from *Façade*) the "hard and braying light" is conceived as "zebra'd black and white."

The "dominions" of "darkeness and light," the witness to the polarity and variety of phenomena are of continuing concern to Edith Sitwell the poet and critic. They are of such importance, in fact, that it is their many powers—begetting of both death and life, "azoic" and vital—which generate and support her conceit of "shadow" that appears to be her most resonant symbol of the unity of being which her poetry seeks to achieve and describe.

NOTHING THAT we have seen of Edith Sitwell's work should lead us to expect that in her poetry the "shadow" or "shade" with which she characterizes the "complete and rounded world" embracing both "darkenesse and light" is an image of tranquilizing contentment. As remarked in the first chapter, her opposing prides of "besetting virtue" and "besetting sin" do not disarm each other: they coexist in the sort of resolution that obviously is not pacification. The "shadow" of Sitwell's poetry, like her pride (and perhaps everything about her), reveals no simplistic acceptance of the proverbial "happy medium."

It is true, however, that in a few instances Miss Sitwell's use of "shadow" appears to suggest an idyllic state. She does, for example, occasionally employ "shadow" as a "fair nurse," in a way similar to that of a brief lyric which she has anthologized several times, George Peele's "Bethsabe's Song."

> *Hot sun, cool fire, tempered with sweet air,*
> *Black shade, fair nurse, shadow my white hair:*
> *Shine sun, burn fire; breathe, air, and ease me;*
> *Black shade, fair nurse, shroud me and please me:*
> *Shadow, my sweet nurse, keep me from burning,*
> *Make not my glad cause, cause of mourning.*
> > *Let not my beauty's fire*
> > *Inflame unstaid desire,*
> > *Nor pierce any bright eye*
> > *That wand'reth lightly.*[1]

Peele's "shade" or "shadow" indeed appears protective
and even pacifying in its ability to "ease," "please," aid a
"glad cause," and be a "sweet" as well as a "fair nurse."
Similarly, in the early poem "The Child Who Saw
Midas" [2] Edith Sitwell recalls how "At the hot sand's edge
. . . our nurses sat,"

> And they were black with shade, and so we named
> Them Asia, Africa, and still they seem
> Each like a continent with flowers and fruits
> Unknown to us; in the hot noon they glistened
> With wild dew crying of some long-still dream.

The setting appears idyllic, and her shadowed repose
seems final,

> Our nurses called to us, their faces lovely
> As that dove-soft hour we call good-night.
> . . . .
> Life was so beautiful that shadow meant
> Not death, but only peace, a lovely lulling.

Yet, as elsewhere in Sitwell's early poetry, one must be
careful not to state categorically that she is writing simply
of a garden paradise, sunny or shady. For the nurses,
although their faces were "lovely as that dove-soft hour we
call good-night," warned

> Oh never
> Must you wander far into the forests
> Lest you should learn life from the dwarfish dust
> The speech of birds and serpents in that glade
> Where we have spoken with the ultimate Darkness—
> . . . .
> For there is one dark forest—one whose name
> You know not, haunted by a darker shade.

When after this admonition life becomes "so beautiful"
that "shadow meant/Not death, but only peace, a lovely
lulling," it is largely because "death" had been warded off.
In this childhood realm, "peace" and "lulling" are clearly
established through contrast; the paradise of Troy Park,
like that of another Paradise, another Troy, in recollection
is seen in the perspective of evil and crumbling ruin.

The "sweet" nursing "shadows" of Troy Park ultimately, then, cannot be taken out of context to illustrate only the existence of absolute happiness. As in "Bethsabe's Song," where "Black shade" is welcomed primarily as protection and surcease from "burning," the "peace" and "lovely lulling" of the shadow in "The Child Who Saw Midas" is completely felt only in contrast to (and in a sense achieved in spite of) the "serpents" of "the ultimate Darkness." If it is "idyllic," it is so largely because it is, in fact, a refuge of contentment, and the conclusion of this poem, leaving us in isolation with a "shadow" of "lovely lulling" is too serene, the confrontation with darker opposition is too definitively avoided to represent adequately Sitwell's symbolist realization of the image of "shadow." A more appropriate description of her symbol is given by her phrase "prophetic shadows" from the poem "The Pleasure Gardens," which concludes the early collection *Troy Park*.

In this poem Sitwell sees as "our own prophetic shadows" "The old Bacchantes of the suburbs" who "sit/-Where sunlight wraps their unloved bones with warmth" and "stare like the dead." The terror of this vision is cathartic, the prophecy instructs, and the poem concludes with the speaker transformed in "summer weather . . . once more young . . . lovely now." The conclusion, however, is not the delusive "lulling" of "The Child Who Saw Midas." The "summer weather" of "Pleasure Gardens" is "unknown and flashing"—presumably touched with storm—and the kind of peace achieved provokes wonder not "lulling."

> Oh, the strange people . . . the child paladins
> From some fantastic delicate pilgrimage.

And most significantly, the final lines leave us with a sense of gestation and revelation.

> The young mamas with shadows lengthening
> Into great birds that sing among the gardens
> Songs from some far-off land,—the distant music!

Both shadows in this poem—those of the "old Bacchantes" and the "young"—are "prophetic," that is, they permit the poet's imaginative "lengthening." It is this extension that is the essence of Sitwell's symbolist use of "shadow."

The poet's most important theme is that expressed in the recurrent line (of "Metamorphosis," "Green Song," and "Prothalamion")

Summer breaks from a long-shadowed kiss.

The shadow of "only peace, a lovely lulling," establishing a retreat from the "ultimate Darkness," would not suggest the opposing realities of "darkenesse and light" out of which Sitwell constructs her meaning in these later poems. The "lovely lulling" of the earlier poem suppresses the darker forces suggested by "shadowed" and fails to contribute to the sense of harmonic tempering which, as the explication of "The Avenue" made evident, is central to Sitwell's work. "Shadow" is meaningful to Sitwell precisely because it can be a symbol of complexity and relationship: as she reiterates in a number of poems, it encompasses an "empire."

Edith Sitwell's satiric use of the nursemaid image on the *Wheels* 1916 cover, and her antecedent depreciation of narrow, suppressive guardianship in the important poem "Pedagogues" appear to be a part of her ultimate rejection of the "lulling" attribute of nursemaid-shade. She does not cultivate that which "lulls" or "overruns." Her dedication is to poetry as a productively meaningful design of "beast and flower," of "darkenesse and light." Rejecting the "blissful light" of Chaucer, her cry (from "Song For Two Voices") is "O Darkness—O Ripeness!" Like Andrew Marvell, a poet for whom she confesses a "peculiar personal passion," [3] she does not praise the superficial pursuit. Progressing as Marvell in "The Garden" from a kind of "narrow verged shade," she too establishes a variety of "green shade" symbolic of the generative spirit's "longer flight."

Writing of the poet's vision, Edith Sitwell has said that "the poet, like the painter, harmonizes what seems to the 'Vegetative Eye' irreconcilable aspects of the world, into a great design, a great balance." [4] Such a "balancing" of the "irreconcilable" is clearly analogous to the inspiration to seventeenth-century metaphysical poetry. Sitwell's harmonizing process has analogy with Crashaw's design of "sweet contest" and "kind contrarietyes." [5] The sustaining conceit of her work, thematic and formal, is a kind of *discordia concors*, and various critics—among them, Joseph Duncan, Kenneth Clark, and Jack Lindsay—have placed her, in Sir Kenneth's phrase, "with the religious poets of the seventeenth century." [6] Mr. Duncan, who observes that "Edith Sitwell exhibited very much a seventeenth-century approach to correspondences," [7] urges "an investigation of the poet's use of metaphysical techniques" to give a "new insight into [her] poetry" (p. 5). "It was partly," he writes in his *Revival of Metaphysical Poetry*, "Dame Edith Sitwell's long affinity with the metaphysicals and the seventeenth century that gave a rare blend of toughness and poignancy to her finest poems" (p. 193).

The preceding chapter presented the parallel treatment of light and darkness by Sitwell and several metaphysical writers of the seventeenth century, but perhaps an even more exact relationship can be demonstrated with "shadow," for Sitwell's connection, through "shade," to Marvell is unequivocally stated. Having praised in 1930 his "The Garden" for "its . . . rich sun and richer shade," [8] a few years later she spoke of her own poetry as "a green thought in a green shade." [9] This interest in Marvell was a lasting one; the opening lines of "Gardeners and Astronomers" (1953),

> *Where the green airs seem fanning palms*
> > *and the green psalms*
> *Of greater waters, where the orange hangs*
> > *huge as Orion*
> *and day-long great gauds and lauds of light*

strongly suggest that "Bermudas" is their provenance.

It is significant that Edith Sitwell described the world of Marvell's "Garden" as one of "rich sun and richer shade," therein perceiving that, although a "happy Garden-state" it is also a complex one and not a simplistic paradise. Withdrawing from an active but shallow society, that of the "busie Companies of Men," equated with the "short and narrow" shade of a "single Herb or Tree," Marvell describes the more various realm of "Fair quiet . . . And Innocence." In "delicious Solitude" there is the "wond'rous Life" of sensuous appeasement in which

> Ripe apples drop about my head,
> The luscious Cluster of the Vine
> Upon my Mouth do crush their Wine
> The Nectaren, and curious Peach,
> Into my hands themselves do reach;

but there is also the life of the "Mind" which

> Mean while . . . from pleasure less,
> Withdraws into its happiness.

It is the Mind which

> creates, transcending these,
> Far other Worlds, and other Seas:
> Annihilating all that's made
> To a green Thought in a green Shade.

This recognition of the complexity of man's nature and life indeed accords with much that can be found in Sitwell's assertion of contrast, diversity, and harmony. In one of her early poems, "Green Geese" (1921), she honors a duality similar to Marvell's, acknowledging that

> Without our Flesh we cannot see

as well as insisting that

> The Spirit, too, must be fed, be fed.

More importantly, Marvell's "Garden" appears to earn her accolade of "richer shade," because the life of the Soul—besides being a higher life literally and figuratively ("My Soul into the boughs does glide")—is clearly a life of continuing ascent. Much that Sitwell demands of the imaginative life in terms of "infinite germination" and "growth of consciousness" is also assumed by Marvell, and, furthermore, the soul's transcendence and preparation "for longer flight" is accomplished within and associated with "green shade."

Marvell's use of "green" to describe a condition of imaginative generation is reinforced with masterful subtlety by his adjective "various" in the lines,

> *And, till prepar'd for longer flight*
> *Waves in its Plumes the various Light.*

The word at first seems to be inconsistent with the stated condition of "all that's made" being annihilated "To a green Thought in a green Shade." If all (including the light) is green, "various Light" seems contradictory. "Various," however, appears to embody a pun on the French *vert* (green) so that, as heard, "various" conveys the meaning of "green-ish" (*vert*-ious) as well as "several." With this reading the word "various" becomes a brilliant conceit of the many-in-one. As such it has an important function in characterizing Marvell's witty realm where the single and unvarying (all is annihilated to "green") fosters continuing generation ("longer flight").

Similarly, the presence of "silver Wings" does not, after analysis, contradict the domination of "green." Not only would the metallic silver take on a green cast or "shade" in the presence of the verdant or "various" color, but more importantly, "silver" also contains within it a pun of *silva* which word without question, connotes the verdant and "green." In "silver," once again Marvell's conceit is ironic and in its subtle allusiveness resolving of contradition or discord.

Reading Sitwell's poetry in the light of her own references to Marvell there is to be noted in her *Sleeping Beauty* an instance of "silver shade,"

> *Time taps at the lovely sylvan trees.*
> *Now underneath the shadows fallen from these*

> *The queen sits with her court, and through the glade*
> *The light from their silks casts another silver shade,*

which in its context following "sylvan" may employ the association of Marvell's "Garden." More certainly, her verse from "Metamorphosis" (1929),

> *Into this green world the melons' dogskin flowers,*
> *Leaves green as country temples, snare the hours*

recalls the poet who stumbled on "melons," who was "insnar'd with flow'rs," and whose garden and green world was much involved with time and hours. Considering her statements about Marvell, her frequent use of "green shade" and other imagery which recall his poetry there seems to be little question about her explicit engagement with Marvell's work—a relationship which confirms and informs her own complexly conceited vision.

Sitwell's first employment of "green shade" appears to be in "The Man with the Green Patch" of 1925. In that poem the old man's patch is twice described as

> *The green shade of Death's own yew-tree*

in which description "green shade" represents not only the omnipresence but also ironically the vitality of death. "Green shade" in this ambivalent context recalls Marvell's irony of finding fertility or the verdant through death or annihilation. In "Romance" (1933) amidst a "country paradise" with fountains and melons and a concern for time that again recalls Marvell, Sitwell describes the state of lovers as

> *Green were the pomp and pleasure of the shade*
> *Wherein they dwelt.*

Love with all its possibilities of the renewing kiss is

> *This empire of green shade.*

But love in "Romance" (as the reader will remember from the previous discussion of the poem's associative technique of "shadowing") wanes, and the tone of the work ultimately is somewhat different from Marvell's "Garden." Despite the poet's stated and obvious debt to Marvell, it becomes evident as one reads her work that the presentation of Sitwell's "green thought in a green shade" is different from Marvell's.

In "The Garden" if there is an allusion to diminution or death in "Shade" it is primarily confined to the "short and narrow verged Shade" of the opening section. The beginning of the poem appears to use little, if any, suggestion of "Shade" as spirit or as a desirable environment for the soul as there is in the later establishment of a "green Thought in a green Shade." And conversely, in the later stanza there seems to be little or no evocation of terror or fear which might be suggested by the relevance of "Shade" to loss or death. Although there is, of necessity some comparison (of contrast) by the reader between the "green Shade" of "longer flight" and that which was "short and narrow verged," the dominant feeling is that the poet with his reader has passed into a different (and higher) realm effectively distinguished from "the busie Companies of Men."

Although in at least one of her poems — "A Young Girl" (1944) — Edith Sitwell presents "green shade" as largely of a "happy Garden-state," more typically, as in "The Man With the Green Patch" and "Romance," she employs the imagery of shadow, including "green shade," in a manner seemingly calculated to accommodate a large measure of multiple allusion.

"A Young Girl" describes the "green shadow of spring" as

> *bringing light to the lonely:*
> *Till the people in islands of loneliness cry to the*
> *other islands*
> *Forgetting the wars of man and of angels, the new Fall*
> *of Man.*

Here, Sitwell's "green shade" appears to be as exact as Marvell's designation of a single region or level of the complex world which he conceives. In this poem Sitwell describes — as more typically she does not — a region "as pure as the Lily born with the white sun," in which state the "Fall of Man," like "narrow verged shade," is forgotten or left behind "for longer flight." At other times, as we shall see below, Edith Sitwell will present an equally unqualified opposing dimension of the loss and diminution suggested by the image of "shadow" or "shade."

Usually, however, as I have emphasized, the imagery of shade is employed in a manner that exploits a depth and range of meaning. Even in a poem like "Most Lovely Shade" (1942) which praises the "Most Lovely Dark" and the "shade's richest splendor" there is important qualification of the dominion of "lovely shade." The resulting special shade is, in particular, not "lulling," nor does it seek to forget the past.

In asking the "shade" (of "Most Lovely Shade"), that "Ethiopia," to

> Come then, my pomp and splendor of the shade
> Most Lovely cloud that the hot sun made black
>   As dark-leaved airs—
>   Come then, O precious cloud,
>   Lean to my heart

the poet recalls (as elsewhere in the poem) the repeated phrases "pomp and pleasure of the shade" of "Romance." The concluding statement of "Most Lovely Shade,"

> No shade of a rich tree
> Shall pour such splendor as your heart to me,

in fact, is a "shadow" or unique Sitwellian repetition of the lines from "Romance,"

> No shade of some rich tree
> Shall pour such splendor as your heart to me.

The author, moreover, in a footnote in her *Collected Poems* instructs the reader, "For a later variation of this Song ["Romance"] . . . see 'Most Lovely Shade.'" With such direction, a reader of the later poem can hardly divorce from his reading of that poem the sense of loss developed in the earlier work.

Love, then, is enhanced in a world of flux; perhaps in a Shakespearean sense: in the presence of shadow's manifestation of life and death one "learns to love that well which thou must leave ere long." With the support of this theme—overt in "Romance"—a fuller reading of "Most Lovely Shade" is realized. For example, with such a reference the description at the midpoint of the poem of the death of Syrinx and Dryope,

Most lovely Shade . . . Syrinx and Dryope
And that smooth nymph that changed into a tree
Are dead

indeed becomes central to the meaning of the work. Continuing, we read that

the shade, that Ethiopia, sees
Their beauty make more bright its treasuries

and realize that it is in large measure because of the death of Syrinx and Dryope that their remembered beauty can "make more bright" the "treasuries" of the Shade.

Edith Sitwell once wrote that "all great poetry is dipped in the dyes of the heart," [10] a statement that well embodies in pun her consistent confrontations with death. Her recurrent imagery of "shadow" is her most effective conceit of resolving the omnipotence of death. Although Marvell uses his "green Shade" as part of a complex world and Sitwell is obviously in debt to him, they are different kinds of poets. In brief, she is a symbolist. Marvell's wit and logic are of a "tough reasonableness," as Eliot has appositely remarked. Sitwell, as a symbolist, is less precise and usually assigns definition to her language with less rigor. She has told us that she seeks "infinite germination for each word"; as a symbolist she suggests and alludes. Marvell's subtlety and complexity, no less admirable, is nonetheless of a different order. In describing Marvell's Mower, Edward Tayler illuminates this distinction. "The Mower is symbolic but not Symbolist," he writes, "for the meanings clustered around Marvell's mysterious figure, while in the last analysis indefinable, are in an important sense neither vague nor illimitable but retain by association something of the firm outline characteristic of their theological formulation." [11]

Both poets recognize a high order of complexity in theme and expression. Marvell speaks at least of three levels of existence in "The Garden": that of worldly affairs (rejected), of the senses (transcended) and of the mind and soul. But his treatment of these is more reasonable—it recalls the incisive and relentless logic, the "Had we . . . But . . . Now" sequence, of his "Coy Mistress," rather than Sitwell's symbolist fusion. "Green Shade" in Marvell's "Garden" describes the fertile realm of thought, whereas in Sitwell's "Green Patch" it describes not only the color of the eye patch, but it also concurrently alludes to death's inevitability, the eternality of death and the metaphysical possibilities that arise out of and in spite of death. The "green shade of Death's own yew-tree" both terrifies and inspirits. And the ultimate ascendency in "The Man With the Green Patch" of hope,

> Come softly and we will look through
> The windows from this avenue. . . .
> For there my youth passed like a sleep,
> Yet in my heart, still murmuring deep,
> The small green airs from Eternity,
> Murmuring softly, never die,

apparently in Sitwell's esthetic is satisfying because of that tension.

The example of "The Garden" affords an excellent demonstration of the meaningful comparison between these two poets. It is difficult to conceive of a careful study of Edith Sitwell's poetry without reference to Marvell and other metaphysical poets. That study, as Joseph Duncan remarked, certainly gives us "new insights into [her] poetry," insights that establish her work ultimately in its own symbolist individuation.

Sitwell's relationship to Crashaw, suggested at the outset of this chapter, must also be qualified. Horace Gregory has noted a close affinity between Crashaw and what he calls Sitwell's "baroque temper." [12] But Duncan presents a different view in stating that Sitwell "herself has shown no real interest in his [Crashaw's] poetry" (p. 193). She had, of course, anthologized his poetry which in a sense is some kind of "real interest," but I believe that Duncan is more correct in limiting Crashaw's influence on Sitwell despite some undeniable similarities.

Regardless of how grotesque a conceit of Crashaw's may be, as in ["Luke 11"],

> Suppose he had been Tabled at thy Teates,
> Thy hunger feels not what he eates:

Hee'l have his Teat e're long (a bloody one)
The Mother then must suck the Son

there is, nonetheless, more definitive concord here (and throughout his work) than in Sitwell's symbolist work. Crashaw's resolving meter and rhyme support the precise logical and theological argument (that the body of Christ in becoming Mother Church then would be capable of nursing) which balance the shocking and discordant tendencies of the imagery. Crashaw's "contests," however more grossly ornamented, are nonetheless essentially "sweeter" than Sitwell's; his "contrarietyes" are "kinder." His apostrophe,

> *Substantial shade! whose sweet allay*
> *Blends both the noones of night and day*

(from "Mr. Crashaw's Answer For Hope") is an excellent example of the resolution to be found (and felt) in his poetry. Sitwell's "shade" or "shadow" will predominate as "substantial," but a "sweet allay"—at least in the sense of being a "sweet nurse"—will not be its prevailing symbolic reference.

Her poem "Colonel Fantock" exhibits in three usages of "shadow" the range and importance beyond that of "sweet allay" which she gives to this symbol. "Shadow" is first used in this poem to characterize the power and influence of the poet's great-grandmother, to bring her world into contrast with that of Colonel Fantock's.

> *When night came, sounding like the growth of trees,*
> *My great-grandmother bent to say good-night,*
> *And the enchanted moonlight seemed transformed*
> *Into the silvery tinkling of an old*
> *And gentle music-box that played a tune*
> *Of Circean enchantments and far seas:*
> *Her voice was lulling like the splash of these.*
> *When she had given me her good-night kiss,*
> *There, in her lengthened shadow, I saw this*
> *Old military ghost with May-fly whiskers.*

Compared with the "lengthened" influence or power of the reigning lady, Fantock was a

> *Poor harmless creature, blown by the cold wind,*
> *Boasting of unseen unreal victories*
> *To a harsh unbelieving world unkind.*

And it is the "Circean enchantment," the "lengthened
shadow" of the great-grandmother that represent that
"harsh unbelieving world unkind." "Shadow" here is analogous to the lulling nursemaid shade ("her voice was
lulling") that Sitwell herself has depreciated. This unreal
fixation of life here as in "Pedagogues" and *Wheels,*
where it is satirized, "overruns the universe," and while it
is kind toward the child it constitutes a "harsh" world to
the aged man.

But the influence or "shadow" of the great-grandmother
is not the only quality of life in Troy Park. "There were,"
we learn,

> *haunted summers in Troy Park*
> *When all the stillness budded into leaves;*
> *We listened, like Ophelia drowned in blond*
> *And fluid hair, beneath stag-antlered trees;*
> *Then, in the ancient park the country-pleasant*
> *Shadows fell as brown as any pheasant,*
> *And Colonel Fantock seemed like one of these.*

These "shadows" are more fruitful—they do not reduce
Fantock to a "ghost." Neither in *Hamlet* nor here is
Ophelia's drowning an unproductive death, for

> *Then, in the ancient park the country-pleasant*
> *Shadows fell as brown as any pheasant.*

From this death comes not a mourning dullness: "brown
as any pheasant" is ironic, and the resulting "shadows"
are, like the bird of this conceit, tinged with vibrant color.

Although the atmosphere in which these "shadows"
exist is peaceful,

> *Sometimes for comfort in the castle kitchen*
> *He drowsed, where with a sweet and velvet lip*
> *The snapdragons within the fire*
> *Of their red summer never tire,*

it is not oppressive. "Colonel Fantock liked our company"; the influence of these shadows is imaginative:

> *For us he wandered over each old lie,*
> *Changing the flowering hawthorn, full of bees,*
> *Into the silver helm of Hercules,*
> *For us defended Troy from the top stair*
> *Outside the nursery, when the calm full moon*
> *Was like the sound within the growth of trees.*

"But," the poet ironically reminds us, these "country-pleasant shadows" cannot persist: "Then came one cruel day in deepest June . . . A gay voice . . . said, 'It is Colonel Fantock's age/Which makes him babble.'" Still another kind of shadow—of "Death" rather than "growth"—appears.

> *The poor old man then knew his creeping fate,*
> *The darkening shadow that would take his sight*
> *And hearing; and he thought of his saved pence*
> *Which scarce would rent a grave. . . . That youthful voice*
> *Was a dark bell which ever clanged "Too late"—*
> *A creeping shadow that would steal from him*
> *Even the little boys who would not spell—*
> *His only prisoners. . . . On that June day*
> *Cold Death had taken his first citadel.*

The poet thus has used "Circean," "country-pleasant," and "darkening" shadows to describe and encompass the oppressive, benign, and naturally inevitable in the world of Colonel Fantock. As an image of relationship, in its variety of definition "shadow" becomes symbolic of the mutability and gradation of which life consists. Furthermore, here in the phrasing of "darkening shadow" we may see the mutation from pheasant brown which conveys the sense of symbolist fusion and allusive interaction between these apparently distinguished species. It is such coalescence that Stephen Spender observes and praises in these remarks written on the occasion of Edith Sitwell's death.

> In the long run poems survive not merely because they receive critical approval, but because people fall in love with them. They live because phrases, imagery, music, echoes, the idea of all the poems coalescing into a world single with the poet, hang about our hearts, become part of our lives. When I was 18 I fell in love with Edith

Sitwell's "Colonel Fantock" . . . and I wrote a sonnet "To Edith Sitwell." [13]

I suggest that the symbolist resonance of "shadow" plays an important part in the creation of this vital unity.

In "Street Song" Sitwell acknowledges "the shade" that is "Like the flowering door /That leads into Paradise," but also remarks another kind of shade: "Man's threatening shadow," and this, she writes, "has a changing shape." John Donne, in one of the love songs which Edith Sitwell has called "perhaps the greatest in our language," [14] also observes and annotates the changing shape and meaning of shadows. In "A Lecture Upon the Shadow" the shadows before noon "which we ourselves produc'd" represent a growing love: as the "morning shadowes weare away" the lovers become more themselves. There is less of them for others to see (we recall Donne's interest in not telling "the laity our love"), and their one world becomes more nearly autonomous. At noon what shadows there are

we doe those shadowes tread

and for the lovers "to brave clearnesse all things are re-duc'd." As the sun is above the lovers, so the lovers are above,—and thus sovereign of—their image on the earth, projected to the outside world. But the shadows after noon "grow longer all the day" and "new shadowes make the other way." As one set of shadows indicates the growth of love, and the "full constant light" of noon represents the meridian of love so the lengthening shadows after noon are images of "decay" and "night."

The title of Donne's poem significantly refers to "the Shadow" as a colective entity, although the poet analyzes various shapes and meanings of shadows in the poem. Similarly, Edith Sitwell's symbol of the shadow comprises a wide range of experience. In fact, with Sitwell as with Donne the shadow is important because it possesses a constellation of meanings. Analogous to Donne's interpretation of a shadow's direction, in Sitwell's poem "The Bat" the speaker (Heliogabalusene, the Bat) notes that

life is a matter of which way falls
Your tufted turreted Shade.

Shadow to both these poets is inseparable from and meaningfully related to existence. Sitwell in "Poor Young Simpleton" observes that

> *somnambulists, rope-walkers, argonauts,*
> *Avators, tamers of steel-birds and fugitives*
> *From dream and reality, emigrants, mourners*

and sees

> *each with his Shadow to prove that Man lives!*

In "Lo, This is She That Was the World's Desire" she observes

> *the shadow leaves*
> *The body when our long dark sun has gone. . . .*
> *And this is the winter's Ethiopian clime*
> *Darkening all beauty.*

Donne, in "A Nocturnall upon S. Lucies Day," also with "shadow" proves the presence of inspiration and substance. Where there is "shadow," he writes, "a light and body must be." Donne's self, lost at "her death" is at "the yeares, and the dayes deep midnight," where in the sun's absence he possesses no shadow. Thus, in his conceit he becomes the "Epitaph" of "every dead thing," the "Elixer" of "the first nothing."

In Sitwell's early poem "Spring," as in Donne's "Nocturnall," that which is shadowless also lacks something vital.

> *When spring begins, the maids in flocks*
> *Walk in soft fields, and their sheepskin locks*
> *Fall shadowless,*

and consequently

> *King Midas heard the swan-bosomed sky*
> *Say, "All is surface and so must die."*

The poem evokes, as do many of her early works, especially those of *Façade*, the "glittering," "jangling harsh" superficiality of existence. And what is not accompanied by or touched by shadow is unreal and artificial. In "On the Vanity of Human Aspirations" (*Wheels*, 1921)

"Anne, the goose-girl" who has "goose-brains" is untouched by an "umbrageous tree" which "Ne'er cast a
shadow on her mind." Intelligence as well as vitality is
measured by Sitwell in terms of awareness of relationship:
"shadow" here again is her image of organic relevance.

Edith Sitwell reveals her close interest in Marvell,
Donne, Sir Thomas Browne, Lord Herbert of Cherbury,
and other metaphysical writers in various ways: reference
in her critical writings and *Notebook*, footnotes to her
poetry, and inclusion of their work in her anthologies.
These explicit references confirm the parallels observed
between her work and theirs. But there is one writer with
sympathies close to hers and the metaphysicals, a writer of
whose work she makes no mention and yet whose work I
assume she knew. That writer is her father, Sir George
Reresby Sitwell, who in 1909 (when Edith was, at twenty-two, still at home) published the book *On the Making
of Gardens*, the result of an all-consuming avocation of
philosophizing about and constructing extensive formal
gardens. The book is important because it is the exposition of many principles which accord with those implied
and stated in his daughter's poetry and criticism. A comparison of their work reveals not only parallels but also
constituent differences, both of which, as with the comparison of her with the metaphysicals, reveal and confirm
important insights into her poetry.

In the "Introduction" to the reissue (1951) of Sir
George's book his son Sir Osbert speaks of him as being
part of a "Hortus Conclusus," an observation that may be
as incorrect about the father as it is about the daughter.
Both father and daughter share the distinction of frequently being placed in an enclosed garden world,
whereas, in fact, both insist on the necessity of a comprehensive and large vision. Moreover, the father, as the
daughter in her subsequent work, emphasizes the role of
shadow in his philosophy and creation of a garden.

Sir George writes (p. 17) that

> there is a peculiar fascination in the upward views through
> grate and pillared court and further archway deep in

shadow, across sunny gardens. . . . These long vistas which pierce a succession of buildings and enclosures seem to appeal to the sentiment of power, and there is some mysterious charm in the alternation of light and shadow.

If in these "long vistas" there is nonetheless some advocacy of "a secret garden far withdrawn from the dust and traffic of the street," that "hortus conclusus" is further qualified by his praise of the "great Renaissance garden-makers" (19),

> for it was in poetry, imagination that they reigned supreme . . . they learnt the value of striking contrast; of sudden and thrilling surprise; of close confinement,

but that "close confinement" was developed

> as a prelude to boundless freedom; of scorching sun as a prelude to welcome shade.

The apparent equation of "boundless freedom" to "welcome shade" offers a striking analogy of the degree and range of experience which Edith attributes to her symbolism of "shadow."

In describing various gardens of Italy, Edith's father continually speaks of the necessity of extending vistas rather than confining them. Of one garden he notes that "turning one's chair, one may look out over the vast stretches of the Campagna" (p. 22). On another, at Mondragone, he rejoices that "after so much gloom and confinement, as you step out upon it ["a little iron balcony"] the boundless view takes your breath away" (p. 24). "The spirit of man," he asserts, "will not be pent up in a narrow compass nor be content without a spacious horizon in which the eye may wander and fancy and memory may move. There is narrowness and madness in these shut-in views" (p. 26). His summation, categorically rejecting the concept and fact of the "hortus conclusus" is that

> The garden must be considered not as a thing by itself, but as a gallery of foregrounds designed to set off the soft hues of the distance.

Of relevance to the garden poetry of the symbolist Edith Sitwell is Sir George's belief (p. 27) that

> It may be argued further that real beauty is neither in garden nor landscape, but in the relation of both to the individual, that what we are seeking is not only a scenic setting for pool and fountain and parterre, but a background for life.

Edith's attention to symmetry and repetition, related, as I have suggested throughout this study, to her concern with "shadow" and "shade" is recalled by her father's comment that the "symmetry and repetition, as at Blickling, will give breadth and repose to a rich façade" (p. 30). He perceives the use of repetition in an organic design (p. 31).

> To the house the garden will be as intimately related for it should be convenient as if one were "stepping from one room to another," and will often carry forward the main divisions or repeat the minor architectural features of the *façade*.

The father's concern for "façade" suggests that Edith's denunciation of the superficial (of no organic depth), especially in her own important work, *Façade*, may derive in part at least from his insistence in executing and describing gardens that appearances and façades be integral and organic and not unrelated to their setting. His remarks on artificial rivers are particularly illuminating (p. 47).

> It has been observed of the sham rivers introduced into English parks by Capability Brown, that when once the two ends have been discovered, they have lost for ever their beauty and their power to please.

Sir George's vision of shadow, however, is—as Marvell's—different from Edith's resonating symbolist realization. Shadow to the father is more like the "fair" and "sweet nurse" of Peele's "Bethsabe's Song." Moreover, in stressing that no discordant note shall be heard in the ideal garden, he reveals his anti-religious feeling (p. 34),

No sound of the outer world should break the enchantment, nor could one silence it, should there vibrate
through the garden the menacing voice of the church bell,
with its muttered curse on nature and on man, lest it beat
down the petals of the pagan roses.

And yet as one rightly perceives that there could be here
no genesis of Edith's work except in reaction, a reader
comes upon further remarks of the father's which seem
eminently consonant with the daughter's later views. For
example, there is little in the following passage (pp.
35–38) that might not be attributed to her.

But if we are to call up this new world of mists and
shadows to replace the illusions of the old, it will be
necessary to . . . analyze the pleasure which the beauty
gives. There is no truth but the whole truth concerning an
object, both in its countless aspects and manifold relations,
and what we call the garden is only a single, fugitive
appearance, an infinitesimal part of the whole. . . . There
is the pride of the eye in colour and curving lines and
dappled light and shade, the suggestion of pleasing rest
and coolness; the intellectual pleasure of the processes of
comparison and deduction: the train of association which
calls up memories of other gardens. . . . Further, there is
the gratification of the instinctive sympathy of reason,
where the scene has the qualities of appropriateness,
diversity in unity, proportion, symmetry or balance, or-
derly progression, all of which come under the head of
design, or at least of order and fitness. In every well-
planned garden, as indeed in every art, there are many
harmonies of appropriateness—in relation, convenience,
proportion or scale, form, colour, historic style—so subtle
as to escape individual notice.

The fact that Edith Sitwell prefers to quote Coleridge and
others on the substance of the above passage does not
prove that in these matters the father had no influence on
the daughter. The evidence of his book suggests that at
least some of her esthetic disposition may derive from
him.

And further, the young woman who a few years after
the appearance of her father's book would discover and

read with avidity the French symbolists and herself begin a symbolist career might well have been interested in this analysis of symbolic suggestion which brings even literature into the garden (p. 43).

> The higher centers of sensations in the cerebral hemispheres are storehouses of old impressions, and those which have often been in action together become connected. . . . Let a fresh cluster of a kind already known unexpectedly, offer itself,—say the view of a garden—and the recognition of it as belonging to a particular class will involve the faint revival in memory or idea of (1) the aggregate of past impressions, and (2) the knowledge grouped about them; in this case all that gardens have meant to countless generations of universal symbol of beauty and motive of ornament, the pathos of the faded rose, the Idyll of Ausonius and Ben Jonson's rendering of it, the garden lore of Herrick, Vaughan, and Herbert, the flower imagery of Milton and Shakespeare, of Keats and Shelley. These ideas, or others like them, will be in the background of consciousness, not in the focus of intellectual sight but in the "fringe" or "halo" of obscurely felt relations; belonging rather to feeling than to knowledge; below the horizon themselves, but rolling up above it a mist of sentiment out of which at any moment trains of conscious throught may spring.

In remembering Sir George, as Dame Edith does, only for the follies he committed in raising her—especially his insistence on a painful and humiliating apparatus [15] to straighten her body and nose—we may do him injustice. *On the Making of Gardens* reveals the father who was a sensitive reader of William James as indeed a remarkable and talented person who may well have given his daughter a legacy other than his alleged contempt.

Sir George, like his daughter, emphasizes in his book "a harmony of contrast," "unity in diversity," and, in a tone and language indistinguishable from hers, appreciates "that great rhythm of harmonic change through birth and death to birth again which is the heart-beat of the universe" (p. 56). "To make a great garden," he instructs, "one must have a great idea" (p. 63). Although his own vision of a garden seems to have been more like the "sweet allay" of Crashaw than the more symbolist and complex one of his daughter, his own idea, if not "great" was not narrow or mean. His advocacy of Le Notre's rule of contrast, "in every corner of the grounds, grouping together sunshine and shadow, grove and bowling-green, high and low, rich and simple, line and curve" (p. 61), while literally related to horticultural effects also figuratively enables and encompasses Edith's later and greater diversities of Christ and Judas, Dives and Lazarus, suffering and joy. It is not difficult to assent to his own statement that "the builder" of "such a garden" as he describes is "like a great poet" (p. 68). The likeness is too close to Edith to be denied or neglected.

Assuming the unlikely possibility that Edith had not read her father's published book of 1909, she certainly had "read" the "great idea" of his vision in the world of "Renishaw" where she spent most of the first third of her life.[16] For it was there on his Derbyshire estate that Sir George assiduously designed and made extensive gardens and landscapes. The chapter "A World of Shadow" of *Taken Care Of* records the weight of that environment (p. 178).

> Every day, unless the grey prison bars of the rain were so thick that we must remain indoors, we sat in the porch of Renishaw, on the north side of the dark and shadowed house. There was nothing to look at, excepting the far brightness of two cornfields, and some magnificent trees, whose shadow seemed always to be upon our house. Indeed, we were like people who walk for ever under the shadow of immemorial trees.
>
> But on the south side are the large and sunny gardens, warmth and clouds of odour and of colour, and bees so like the warm and buzzing lights, bee-winged light so like the honey-makers, that one could hardly know one from the other. The enormous elms of the avenue shed now their green and golden dust, the fantasies splash, the eternal statues have forgotten everything that was mournful in their past.

Her observations here that "ours was a world of shadow, and of unmistakable shadows" indicates how, to her death, "shadow" was an integral part of her life. Her subsequent discussion in this very brief chapter (five pages) of her themes of suffering and redemption especially in the poem "The Shadow of Cain" (1947) indicates also how much she associates the world of shadow at Renishaw with her poetic life.

If her own and others' anecdotes of her life reveal that she scorned her father, her poetry attests that nonetheless she came to use imaginatively much that had been his own consuming passion. It may even be reasonable to suggest that, believing she had been denied her father's love—figuratively excluded from his garden for her crooked nose and ungainly form (she did not "fit in" with the beautiful)—she widened her own poetic vision of beauty to include even the crooked. For it is in the charity and comprehension of the unique garden of her poetry that in "Old Woman" (of *Street Songs*) "the crooked have a shadow light made straight" and in "Out of School" (of *Gardeners and Astronomers*) "the shadows of the crooked and straight complete each other."

This comprehension and "richer shade" of Edith Sitwell's poetic world—which is to a considerable degree a garden world of metaphysical comprehension—is not generally recognized, especially in the early poetry. Concerning that work, Mr. J. I. M. Stewart has written (*Eight Modern Writers*, pp. 16–17) that

> In the year following *The Waste Land* she published *Bucolic Comedies*, so that we all at that time, when we had had enough of Madame Sosostris and the Phoenician Sailor would turn to chanting about Lily O'Grady silly and shady, and her decorative, if obscure connexion with Calliope, Io, Pomona, Antiope, Echo, and Clio. . . .

Like Philip Toynbee, who in reviewing *Taken Care Of*, deftly "takes care of" Dame Edith by remarking,

> I am sure that she had, in her early years, genuine and original talent for the writing of light verse,[17]

Stewart persists in seeing only half of Sitwell's vision. Actually, as Yeats understood, and as I have earlier quoted, her "dream is double." "In its first half," Yeats observes, "she creates . . . an elegant, artificial childhood," but concurrently in the other half, driven by "a necessity of contrast" there is "a nightmare vision like that of Webster, of the emblems of mortality." [18]

One of Sitwell's "emblems of mortality,"—the chief one, I submit—is "shadow," and it is noteworthy that Stewart in characterizing the "decorative" nature of the early poetry cites "Lily O'Grady, silly and shady" (from "Popular Song").[19] For the "decorative" nature of the early work is significantly qualified by "shady," and the contrasting juxtaposition "silly and shady" is an effective one throughout the early work. Its main conceit is that of "terrible gaiety."

The depth and range of meaning that Edith Sitwell evokes from Lily O'Grady—beyond that of "silly" and decorative relief from Eliot—could be inferred from Sitwell's association of her with Calliope, Io, Pomona, Antiope, Echo, and Clio. Lily O'Grady, aside from being "silly," shadows all the past and experience suggested by those names. "Silly," in this context of pastoral allusion, also carries the meaning of "unsophisticated." In this presentation Sitwell seems to be demanding too much, too rapidly from the reader, and I think that this particular passage fails. The connection of Madame Sosostris with the sibyl of Cumae and the women of "The Burial of the Dead" is much more effectively developed. But rather than creating simply an antidote to *The Waste Land* Sitwell has striven to incorporate a vision analogous to that poem's in her own satirically "light" one. Whereas Madame Sosostris is only "shady," Sitwell attempts a character both "shady" and "silly." Edith Sitwell, who in 1920 denounced the "petits bonheurs" of the British music hall, has not in "Popular Song" produced a "tin-pan alley" antithesis to *The Waste Land*. The poem, in fact, ends with a perception entirely consonant with that of Eliot's poem,

> *And shade is on the brightest wing,*
> *And dust forbids the bird to sing.*

"Shade" in this context, as in qualifying Lily O'Grady, is evocative of an extensive range and depth of association.

One of the many poems that were published in *Bucolic Comedies* having deceptively rustic titles and appearing to be an antidote to the arid world of Eliot's is "Spinning Song." But although the opening is indeed happily bucolic,

> *The Miller's daughter*
> *Combs her hair*
> *Like flocks of doves*
> *As soft as vair . . .*

we soon learn that "those soft flocks flutter down/Over the empty grassy town." And although the miller's daughter is "Like a queen in a crown/Of gold light, she/Sits neath the shadows'/Flickering tree." Under a surface "gaiety" (which ultimately becomes a kind of "terrible gaiety") we find that Mrs. Grundy is "malicious." And the miller's daughter finds little frivolity or comedy in her bucolic life, for "her heart is heavy as bags of gold," a simile revealing the ironic disposition of Edith Sitwell. The concluding lines—"heavy" as well as "light"—are,

> *For everything comes to the shadows at last*
> *If the spinning-wheel Time move slow or fast.*

Even the poem "Spring" from *Bucolic Comedies* hardly gives us a green and pleasant relief from Eliot's desiccation. This poem describes not Chaucer's "Aprille" filled with "blissful light," but Eliot's "cruellest month." When in the "shadowless" land King Midas (as we saw above) hears the "swan-bosomed sky"

> *Say, "All is surface and so must die,"*

we recognize the theme of "The Burial of the Dead": that our anxious society endures a living death by refusing to accept and comprehend the full realities of life and death. The recognition of life-in-death, the actuality and inspiration of "shadow" wanting, "Spring" understandably concludes with

> *the leaping goat-footed waterfalls*
> *Singing their cold-forlorn madrigals.*

One of those songs—I might speculate—could appropriately be *Oed' und leer das Meer* from *The Waste Land*.

Although it is distorting to make an absolute dichotomy between Edith Sitwell's "early" and "late" poetry, it is possible and necessary to distinguish the degree of change that does exist. The development of her imagery of "shadow," moreover, suggests the nature of the difference between what are often termed her "decorative" and "mature" periods. In her poem "A Hymn to Venus" of 1947 Edith Sitwell uses the important and revealing phrase "the Shadow's treasury," and in that reference is manifest the change in attitude toward life and society that Sitwell underwent after 1929. As I have demonstrated, from her very first published poems she employed the imagery of light and darkness, particularly of shadow with a symbolic awareness of its role in describing the presence or absence of a viable and complex vision. But much of her early work like that of *Bucolic Comedies* and *Façade* up to and including *Gold Coast Customs* of 1929 is satiric. As "Pedagogues," "The Avenue," and *Wheels* indicate she was engaged in denouncing trite and simplistic Victorian poetic modes and encouraging a new avenue of wider comprehension. Her tone in the service of that attack and reform generally is ironic and sharply critical. In this mood "shadow" and "shade" are frequently used to indict society, to allude to a necessary complexity that is missing (as in "Spring") or to suggest the dimension of Cold Death (as in "Spinning Song").

A new emphasis appears to be manifest in the long (and appositely titled) poem "Metamorphosis" of 1929. The change is particularly indicated by the lines,

> *But yet it shall avail that grass shall sing*
> *From loveless bones in some foreshadowed spring.*
> *And summer breaks from a long-shadowed kiss.*

Her attitude throughout this poem is not primarily to expose and attack

> *The terrible Gehenna of the bone*
> *Deserted by the flesh, tears changed to stone,*

but to enunciate more discursively an attitude of inspiriting acceptance. Even though

> *our dry bones are sunless grown as this,*
> *And eyeless statues, broken and alone*
> *In shadeless avenues, the music gone*
> *We stand,*

the poet now, with greater equanimity of tone realizes that

> *Death is our clime*
> *And, among heavy leaves, our bell to chime—*
> *Death is our sun, illumining our old*
> *Dim-jewelled bones.*

In this poem the "shade" is now recognized as "eternal shade" and man is part of a "vast empire of eternal shade." The tone of "Metamorphosis" is more understanding and explicative,

> *Since all things have beginnings: the bright plume*
> *Was once thin grass in shady winter's gloom.*

And this poem casts its special reverberation—its own "shadows"—throughout her subsequent work.

The cause of this change in temperament, if one can be assigned, appears to be a spiritual or religious experience as described in the poem itself,

> *Hate-hidden by a monk's cowl of ape's pelf,*
> *Bear-clumsy and appalling, mine own self*
> *Devouring, blinded by the earth's thick hood*
> *I crouched . . .*
>
> *Then my immortal Sun arose, Heavenly Love,*
> *To rouse my carrion to life and move*
> *The polar night.*

Stephen Spender has written of Edith Sitwell that

> Her poetry is founded on her loves and hates, her sympa-
> thies and prejudices, her miscellaneous reading, and, of
> recent years, on the deepening of her religious faith since
> her conversion to Catholicism.[20]

This "conversion" in 1955 cannot, however, "explain" the
"Metamorphosis" of 1929. But little if anything, in Sitwell
is unforeshadowed, and the formal fulfillment confirms
the existence of beginnings which in her case are most
overt in "Metamorphosis"—although religious and specifically Christian allusion does also antedate that poem. For
example, in "The Man With the Green Patch" of 1925, a
poem suggesting the eternality of the soul, she writes of

> *The shadow of that awful Tree*
> *Cast down on us from Calvary.*

Sir Kenneth Clark also acknowledges the importance of
religion to her, observing at her death, that "in the end
only the Catholic Church saved her from despair." [21] But
this remark, as Spender's, is made about the person who
wrote the poetry and not about the poetry. If such information leads one to find the poems since her conversion
Catholic in spirit, one quickly must admit that they are no
more Catholic than "Metamorphosis" and a whole, vast
shadowed network of poems conceived in the spirit of that
seminal poem between 1929 and 1955—and more than a
few of even the "early" poems.

Moreover, she states in the introduction to her last
collection (*Music and Ceremonies*), the only one issued
after her conversion, that in those poems she is returning
technically to the era of *Façade*. How explain in the light
of her conversion this return to 1922? As I stated in an
earlier chapter, stressing the continuity of her work, such a
return was not really a dislocation at all, because despite
some changes—primarily in the dimunition of the satiric
tone—she is a remarkably consistent poet. The poet of
apparently deepened religious faith after 1955 could "return" to recollect a previous style because even at that
earlier time her spiritual commitment—whatever it might

have been officially—was consonant with her later "con-
verted" position.

After "Metamorphosis" the dominant tone of a Sitwell
poem, with few exceptions, will be to accept and trans-
form with metaphysical conceit and symbolist technique
the "huge weight of centuries" and the "sad eternities" of
"Death's ruined town." Although previous to "Metamorphosis" Edith Sitwell had always indicated a keen awareness of the human condition, there was, beyond a general
but not exclusive use of satire, no consistent manifestation
of what to do about it. Should it be reformed and laughed
at as in *Façade*? Should it be accorded pathos as in "Colonel Fantock"? Or should it be embraced and loved in all
its evil as in "The Mother"? The early poetry is more
tentative in attitude than her later work. But almost nothing that can later be found in her work is missing from her
beginnings except that note of resolved assurance—after
1929—that the extended range of all experience is a "treasury," in particular, the "Shadow's treasury."

As with Marvell and Donne who evaluate the quality of
existence in terms of shadow and shade, Sitwell by embracing life comes to accept shade and all it symbolizes in
"A Tattered Serenade: Beggar to Shadow!" Shade becomes her inseparable companion,

> *I have no friend from whom I must part*
> *But the shade that I cast—my one friend*
> *Till at last the world comes to an end.*

The shadow does indeed copy and therefore inform or
illustrate Man,

> *For face, you have a hollow wolf-gray cowl*
> *Like mine*

and

> *My overcoat, like yours, is an ideal.*

In "Gardeners and Astronomers" (1953) the Shadow is
called the "epitome of our age" which "now rules the

world." Furthermore, in this poem the shadow is Fallen Man,

> *Horizontal Man, the Black Man, who in the Day's*
> *blazing diamond-mine follows the footsteps*
> *Of Vertical Man.*

Inseparable from man, his shadow is ever cast by him

> *Across all growth, all stone.*

No less than Donne, Sitwell lectures upon the shadow, in conclusion finding it (as Horizontal Man)

> *great as Man's ambition,*
> *And like to Man's ambition, with no body*
> *To act ambition—he, the sole horizon.*

"Shadow" like Fallen Man is of this world, but its "treasury" allusively also joins him with spiritual futurity and dimension. Shadow wittily is the "sole horizon," and its "empire" is "eternal."

The theme that underlies all of her work most insistently from "Metamorphosis" on (but the sources of which are clearly to be found in her early work) is that out of "Mankind's dark seedtime"

> *out of the dark, see our*
> *great Spring begins—*
> *Our Christ, the new Song, breaking out*
> *in the fields and hedge rows*
>
> . . . .
>
> *He comes, our Sun, to melt the eternal ice*
> *Of death, the crust of Time round the sunken soul.*

This pervading conceit of suffering leading to spiritual salvation appears to explain why "shadows" as depicted in the locality of "Hell" in her early poems have no generative or fruitful role. In the above lines from the second version of "Metamorphosis" (1946) Sitwell clearly reveals another of her affinities with the metaphysical poets of the seventeenth century: the obvious but frequent pun of Sun and Son (Christ). Since shadows come from the Sun, then they might indeed have no meaningful place in Hell (except to harrow it). In "Singerie" on a "Summer afternoon in Hell" the "shadows" are "louche" or suspicious. In "Mandoline" set "Down in Hell's gilded street" there are

Old shadows bent, alas!

And in "Barber's Shop" Beelzebub's fire "routs shadows." If part of the symbolism of "shadow" suggests the eternal life of the spirit (shade) that grows out of earthly trial, then "shadows," rightfully part of the world, are properly out of place in "Hell," and understandably appear there as anomalous and unwanted. Edith Sitwell's general depiction of "Hell" or the hellish as the undifferentiated and absolute in the early poems which I have explicated contributes to her symbolist realization of "shadow" as manifesting organic complexity.

Although this chapter opened with a qualification of Sitwell's use of "shadow" to evoke a lulling peace, the role of a "sweet nurse," it is obvious that ultimately in its total reference and usage "shadow" does bring a kind of peace and consolation. "The Shadow's treasury" is real and effective; its empire includes its effects: summer and harvest. "The sweet allay" that the symbol of "shadow" represents for Sitwell is, however, not that of an idyllic refuge such as she associates with the nurse-maid world. Her poetry constructs no simplistic "heaven-haven." It embodies the kind of comfort that comes from encountering and confronting experience—joy and suffering, light and darkness, "beast and flower"—and shaping it with poetic and imaginative conceit. In that operation the symbol of "shadow," realized in organization and metaphor, is for Edith Sitwell a central (and perhaps the most important) expression of her unique poetry.

Introduction

1. Stephen Spender, "Images in the Poetic World of Edith Sitwell," *A Celebration For Edith Sitwell*, ed. José Garcia Villa (Norfolk, Conn., 1948), p. 12.

2. *Ibid.*, p. 11., quoted by Spender.

3. *The Oxford Book of Modern Verse*, ed. William Butler Yeats (New York, 1937), p. xviii.

4. C. M. Bowra, "The War Poetry of Edith Sitwell," *Celebration*, p. 20.

5. Donald Davie and Patrick Cruttwell, quoted in John Press, *Rule and Energy* (London, 1963), p. 38.

6. Yeats, *Oxford Book*, p. xviii.

7. Bowra, p. 22.

8. Stephen Spender, *Poetry Since 1939* (London, 1946), p. 20.

9. From the *Literary World*, quoted in *Wheels* (Oxford, 1917), Appendix: "Press Cuttings."

10. From the *Pall Mall Gazette*, quoted in *Wheels* (London, 1920), Appendix: "Press Cuttings."

11. F. R. Leavis, *New Bearings in English Poetry* (London, 1932), p. 73.

12. In this play (1962) Dame Edith is caricatured in the role of Kitty Entrail.

13. Osbert Sitwell, "A Reminiscence" *Celebration*, pp. 9–10. He retells it later in *Noble Essences* (1950), but then omits the details of "isolation" and "rankling." Edith Sitwell herself relates it in *Taken Care Of* (New York, 1965), pp. 19–20.

14. James Dickey, The New York *Times Book Review* (September 1, 1963), p. 5.

15. J. I. M. Stewart, *Eight Modern Writers* (Oxford, 1963), p. 17.

16. Gertrude Stein, "Sitwell Edith Sitwell," *Celebration*, p. 120.

17. For the six years 1960–65 the Bibliographies of the Modern Language Association give only six citations of work in English on Edith Sitwell.

18. As recently as 1963 I did not perceive the unique use of repetition and unitive elements or the "shadows" which are the subject of this study. For my earlier view see James Brophy, "Edith Sitwell: Modern Metaphysical," *Renascence*, xv (Spring, 1963), 152–56.

19. William York Tindall, *The Literary Symbol* (New York, 1955), pp. 12–13.

20. Reuben Brower, *The Fields of Light* (New York, 1962), p. 92.

1 – "Electric Eel"

1. *The Oxford Book of Modern Verse*, ed. William Butler Yeats (New York, 1937), p. xviii.

2. Edith Sitwell, "Pride," *The Seven Deadly Sins* (London, 1962), pp. 15–22.

3. Edith Sitwell, "Drowned Suns," The London *Daily Mirror*, no. 2928 (March 13, 1913), p. 9.

4. Edith Sitwell, "Ezra Pound," *Aspects of Modern Poetry* (London, 1934), pp. 178–214, *passim*.

5. Edith Sitwell, *Atlantic Book of British and American Poetry*, Vol. ii. (London, 1958), p. 993.

6. Samain's original lines (from *Au jardin de l'Infante*),

> *Ton souvenir est comme un livre bien aimé*
> *Qu'on lit sans cesse, et qui jamais n'est refermé*

reveal the sound basis for Sitwell's satiric response.

7. The New York *Times* (December 10, 1964), p. 41.

8. Edith Sitwell, "Preface," *Taken Care Of* (New York, 1965).

9. Edith Sitwell, *Alexander Pope* (New York, 1962). First published in 1930.

10. She even repeats some of this attack in *Taken Care Of*, pp. 170–72.

11. Published in both London and New York in 1965, this "autobiography" is disappointingly slight and repetitive to those who know her work.

12. John Malcom Brinnin, "Thin Facade for Edith Sitwell," *New Yorker* (May 23, 1953), p. 36.

13. Robert Conquest, "Letters to the Editor," London *Times Literary Supplement* (December 19, 1963), p. 1049.

14. Philip Toynbee, "With Malice Toward Some, The London *Observer Weekend Review* (April 4, 1965), p. 27.

2 — *"Taste, Judgment and Kindliness"*

1. Gerard Manley Hopkins, *Poems* (New York, 1948), p. xviii.

2. William York Tindall, *Forces in Modern British Literature 1885–1956* (New York, 1956), p. 284.

3. Edith Sitwell, *A Poet's Notebook* (Boston, 1950) and (London, 1943). The contents of the two editions differ.

4. Quoted by M. H. Abrams, ed., *Norton Anthology of English Literature*, Vol. II (New York, 1962), p. 8.

5. Both essays on Milton may be found in T. S. Eliot, *On Poetry and Poets* (New York, 1957).

6. Edith Sitwell, *Poetry and Criticism* (New York, 1926), pp. 18–19.

7. W. H. Pritchard, *Amherst Alumni Bulletin* (Amherst, 1963), p. 32. (A review of Brower's *The Poetry of Robert Frost*)

8. Reuben Bower, *The Poetry of Robert Frost* (New York, 1963), p. 159.

9. Pritchard, p. 32.

10. Edith Sitwell, *Aspects of Modern Poetry* (London, 1934), p. 105.

11. Reuben Bower, *The Fields of Light* (New York, 1962), p. 61.

12. Cleanth Brooks, *The Well-Wrought Urn* ("The Case of Miss Arabella Fermor").

13. *Ibid.*, p. 87.

14. Regarding her close knowledge of English poetry Edith Sitwell has stated in the *New Age* (August 10, 1922) that "In spite of the general belief that I am a woman of incalculable savagery with only one end in view, that of burning the Library of the British Museum, it is a fact that I have read and know intimately practically all the poetry written in the English tongue since the time of Chaucer."

15. Edith Sitwell, *The Pleasures of Poetry*, Third Series

(London, 1932), p. 3. This anthology was originally published in three separate "series" or volumes. A one-volume combined edition later appeared in 1934.

3—"Shadow" and Internal Order

1. John Lehmann, *Edith Sitwell* (London, 1952).
2. Edith Sitwell, *Collected Poems* (New York, 1954), p. xvi. "Some Notes" is the long prefatory essay.
3. John Crowe Ransom, *The New Criticism* (Norfolk, Conn., 1941), p. xi.
4. A consideration of the two complete lines, "Indianapolis And the Acropolis"—which consideration Sitwell does not make—shows a similar reversal: the second line begins with the "an" sound of the first line's middle.

4—"My Collected Work"

1. This perceptive formulation is from a private conversation with Professor Tindall.
2. Edith Sitwell, *The Pleasures of Poetry*, First Series, (London, 1930), p. 8.
3. Edith Sitwell, *The Pleasures of Poetry*, Second Series, (London, 1931), p. 4. In the *New Age* (July 27, 1922) Edith Sitwell writes of the poetry of Isaac Rosenberg with a similar concern for artistic integrity. "It is almost impossible," she states, "to quote from his work, because the lines lose their savour and their greatness when taken away from the whole."
4. Edith Sitwell, *The Song of the Cold* (London, 1945), p. v.
5. *Music and Ceremonies* published in 1963 is the American edition of *The Outcasts* (London, 1962) to which three poems, including "Music and Ceremonies," were added. "The Outcasts" stands first in both editions.
6. From Sydney Goodsir Smith's *So Late Into the Night* (London, 1952) to which Edith Sitwell wrote the introduction.
7. *The Oxford Book of Modern Verse*, ed. William Butler Yeats (New York, 1937), p. xviii.
8. Horace Gregory, "The 'Vita Nuova' of Baroque Art in the Recent Poetry of Edith Sitwell," *Poetry*, June 1945, p. 148. The reception of Sitwell's poetry in the United States may be indicated by the date of this review. *Street Songs* had been published in England in 1942, and *Green Song* in

1944. *Street Songs* never appeared in an American edition, while *Green Song* was not published in America until 1946.

9. J. I. M. Stewart, *Eight Modern Writers* (Oxford, 1963), p. 17.

10. *Oxford Book*, p. xviii.

11. Jack Lindsay, "The Latest Poems of Edith Sitwell," *A Celebration For Edith Sitwell*, ed. José Garcia Villa (Norfolk, Conn., 1948), p. 47.

12. Ihab Hassan, "Edith Sitwell and the Symbolist Tradition," *Comparative Literature*, VII (Summer 1955), 247.

13. Babette Deutsch, *Poetry in Our Time* (Garden City, 1963), p. 251.

14. Cited by Ralph J. Mills, Jr., "The Poetic Roles of Edith Sitwell," *Chicago Review*, XIV (1961), p. 42.

15. Richard Ellmann and Charles Feidelson, Jr., eds. *The Modern Tradition* (New York, 1965), p. vii.

16. *The American Genius*, ed. Edith Sitwell (London, 1951), preface.

17. E. M. Forster, *Aspects of the Novel* (New York, n.d.), p. 168.

18. Gertrude Stein, "Sitwell Edith Sitwell" *Celebration*, p. 103.

5—The "Dominions" of "Darkenesse and Light"

1. *The Atlantic Book of British and American Poetry*, ed. Edith Sitwell, Vol. I (Boston, 1958), p. 31.

2. *Ibid.*, p. 983.

3. Edith Sitwell, *Children's Tales from the Russian Ballet* (London, 1920), preface.

4. Edith Sitwell, *Atlantic Book*, p. 984.

5. *A Book of the Winter*, ed. Edith Sitwell (London, 1950), p. 10. *A Book of Flowers*, ed. Edith Sitwell (London, 1952), p. 22.

6. Sir Kenneth Clark, "On the Development of Miss Sitwell's Later Style," *A Celebration for Edith Sitwell*, ed. José Garcia Villa (Norfolk, Conn., 1948), p. 56.

7. *Ibid.*, p. 109. In Edith Sitwell's poetry the Lion and the Rose are closely related to the Sun.

8. *Ibid.*, p. 30.

9. "Polka" from *Façade* (London, 1922).

10. "When the Sailor" from *Bucolic Comedies* (London, 1923).

11. "An Old Woman" from *Street Songs* (London, 1942).

12. "Eurydice" from *The Song of the Cold* (London, 1945).

13. C. M. Bowra, "The War Poetry of Edith Sitwell," *Celebration*, p. 31.

14. Ralph J. Mills, Jr., "The Poetic Roles of Edith Sitwell," *Chicago Review*, xiv (Spring, 1961), p. 57.

15. Geoffrey Grigson, "Nothing Like a Dame," *New York Review of Books* (May 20, 1965), p. 11.

16. John Piper, "The Garden and the Harvest," *Celebration*, p. 54.

17. Edith Sitwell, *Rustic Elegies* (London, 1927), p. 83.

18. "The Song of the Beggar Maid to King Cophetua" from Edith Sitwell's *Gardeners and Astronomers* (New York, 1953).

19. Richard Crashaw, "Mr. Crashaw's Answer For Hope."

20. *Pall Mall Gazette* in "Press Notices," *Wheels*, 1916 (second issue, dated 1916, but published April 14, 1917) and *Wheels* 1917.

21. *The Aberdeen Journal, ibid.*

22. *Country Life, ibid.*

23. "Press Notices," *Wheels* 1916 (second issue), and *Wheels* 1917.

24. John McKenna, "The Early Poetry of Edith Sitwell," (unpublished Columbia University dissertation, 1963), p. 153.

25. "Press Notices," *Wheels* 1916 (second issue) and 1917.

26. Katharine Lyon Mix, *A Study in Yellow* (Lawrence, 1960), pp. 2–3.

27. From Robert Frost's "The Oven Bird" in *Mountain Interval* (New York, 1916).

28. It should be noted that Edith Sitwell herself appreciated Frost's poetry. At least, in her introduction to her large anthology, *The Atlantic Book of British and American Poetry* she cites as an "exquisite phrase" Frost's remark that poetry "begins in delight, and ends in wisdom." And she anthologizes eight of his poems including "The Tuft of Flowers"—a relatively large number considering that she includes seven by Gerard Manley Hopkins and three by Wilfred Owen, both poets whom she profusely admired. The discus-

sion of theme here has nothing to do with the achieved organic texture of Frost's style which Sitwell would not have failed to notice (and apparently did not).

29. The poet's own reading of *Façade* on a number of phonograph records is instructive.

6 – "The Empire of Shade"

1. Edith Sitwell's *The Atlantic Book of British and American Poetry*, Vol. 1 (Boston, 1958), p. 177 and her *Planet and Glow-Worm* (London, 1944), p. 1.

2. Edith Sitwell, *Troy Park* (London, 1925), pp. 9–10.

3. *The Pleasures of Poetry*, ed. Edith Sitwell, First Series (1930), p. 40.

4. Edith Sitwell, "Poet's Vision," *Saturday Evening Post* (November 15, 1958), p. 126.

5. Richard Crashaw, "The Weeper" (stanza xvi).

6. Sir Kenneth Clark, "On the Development of Miss Sitwell's Later Style," *A Celebration For Edith Sitwell*, ed. José Garcia Villa (Norfolk, Conn., 1948), p. 66.

7. Joseph E. Duncan, *The Revival of Metaphysical Poetry* (Minneapolis, 1959), p. 193.

8. *The Pleasures of Poetry*, First Series, p. 43.

9. Edith, Osbert, and Sacheverell Sitwell, *Trio, Dissertations on Some Aspects of National Genius* (London, 1938), p. 174.

10. "Poet's Vision," p. 26.

11. Edward Tayler, *Nature and Art in Renaissance Literature* (New York and London, 1964), p. 163.

12. Horace Gregory, "The 'Vita Nuova' of Baroque Art in the Recent Poetry of Edith Sitwell," *Poetry*, LXVI (June 1945), p. 154.

13. Stephen Spender, "Edith Sitwell, Poet," The London *Observer*, December 13, 1964, p. 28.

14. *Atlantic Book*, p. 223.

15. Edith called it her "Bastille."

16. She "left home" and took up residence in London in 1912 when she was 25. She died at the age of 77.

17. Philip Toynbee, "With Malice Toward Some," The London *Observer Weekend Review*, April 4, 1965, p. 27.

18. *The Oxford Book of Modern Verse*, ed. William Butler Yeats (New York, 1937), p. xviii.

19. The poem did not, as Stewart implies, appear in *Bucolic Comedies* (1923). It was first published in 1928, and

in 1930 appeared under the heading "Bucolic Comedies" in *Collected Poems*. Since 1949 the author has included it in her *Façade*.

20. Stephen Spender, "Edith Sitwell, Poet," The London *Observer* (December 13, 1964), p. 28.

21. Sir Kenneth Clark, "The Authentic Sibylline Voice," The London *Times* (December 13, 1964), p. 27.

SELECTED BIBLIOGRAPHY

WORKS ABOUT EDITH SITWELL

Bowra, C. M. *Edith Sitwell*. Monaco, 1947.

——. "The War Poetry of Edith Sitwell," *A Celebration For Edith Sitwell*. Norfolk, Conn., 1948.

Brinnin, John Malcolm. "Thin Façade for Edith Sitwell," The *New Yorker*, xxxix (May 23, 1953), 36.

Brophy, James. "Edith Sitwell: Modern Metaphysical," *Renascence*, xv (Spring 1963), 152–56.

A Celebration For Edith Sitwell. José Garcia Villa, ed., Norfolk, Conn., 1948. (Hereafter called *Celebration*.)

Clark, Sir Kenneth. "The Authentic Sibylline Voice," The London *Sunday Times* (December 13, 1964), 27.

——. "On the Development of Miss Sitwell's Later Style," *Celebration*.

Conquest, Robert. "Poem," The London *Times Literary Supplement* (December 19, 1963), "Letters to the Editor."

Duncan, Joseph E. *The Revival of Metaphysical Poetry*. Minneapolis, 1959.

"Edith Sitwell." The London *Times* (December 10, 1964).

——. The New York *Times* (December 10, 1964).

Fifoot, Richard. *A Bibliography of Edith, Osbert and Sacheverell Sitwell*. London, 1963.

Gregory, Horace. "The Recent Prose and Poetry of Edith Sitwell," *Celebration*.

——. "The 'Vita Nuova' of Baroque Art in the Recent Poetry of Edith Sitwell," *Poetry*, lxvi (June 1945), 148–56.

Green, Timothy. "I am an Electric Eel in a Pool of Catfish," *Life*, liv (January 4, 1963), 60–62.

Grigson, Geoffrey. "Nothing Like a Dame," *New York Review of Books*, IV, 8 (May 20, 1965), 11–12.

Hartley, L. P. "Trends in the Poetry of Edith Sitwell," *Celebration*.

Hassan, Ihab. "Edith Sitwell and the Symbolist Tradition," *Comparative Literature*, VII (Summer 1955).

Lehmann, John. "Edith Sitwell," *Celebration*.

————. *Edith Sitwell*. London, 1952.

Lindsay, Jack. "The Latest Poems of Edith Sitwell," *Celebration*.

McKenna, John Paul. "The Early Poetry of Edith Sitwell" (Unpublished Columbia University Dissertation), 1963.

Mills, Ralph, J. Jr., "The Poetic Roles of Edith Sitwell," *Chicago Review*, XIV (Spring 1961), 31–64.

Pryce-Jones, Alan. "Edith Sitwell," *Commonweal* (May 14, 1965), 241–43.

Sitwell, Sir George Reresby. *On the Making of Gardens*. New York, 1951.

Sitwell, Sir Osbert. *Left Hand, Right Hand!*. Boston, 1944.

————. *The Scarlet Tree*. Boston, 1946.

————. *Great Morning*. Boston, 1947.

————. *Laughter in the Next Room*. Boston, 1948.

————. *Noble Essences*. Boston, 1950.

Spender, Stephen. "Edith Sitwell, Poet," The London *Observer* (December 13, 1964).

————. "Images in the Poetic World of Edith Sitwell," *Celebration*.

————. *Poetry Since 1939*. London, 1946.

Stein, Gertrude. "Sitwell Edith Sitwell" in *Celebration*.

Tindall, William York. *Forces in Modern British Literature, 1885–1956*. New York, 1956.

Toynbee, Philip. "With Malice Toward Some," The London *Observer Weekend Review* (April 4, 1965).

Yeats, William Butler, ed., *The Oxford Book of Modern Verse*. New York, 1937.

WORKS BY EDITH SITWELL

Alexander Pope. New York, 1962.

Aspects of Modern Poetry. London, 1934.

Bucolic Comedies. London, 1923.

Children's Tales from the Russian Ballet. London, 1920.

The Collected Poems of Edith Sitwell. New York, 1954.

Façade. London, 1922.

Five Variations on a Theme. London, 1933.

Gardeners and Astronomers. New York, 1953.

Gold Coast Customs. London, 1929.

Green Song. New York, 1946.

The Mother. Oxford, 1915.

Music and Ceremonies. New York, 1963.

A Notebook on William Shakespeare. Boston, 1962.

The Outcasts. London, 1962.

Poetry and Criticism. New York, 1926.

A Poet's Notebook. London, 1943 and New York, 1950. The contents of the two editions differ.

"Poet's Vision," *Saturday Evening Post* (November 15, 1958), 26–29, 126.

"Pride" in *The Seven Deadly Sins*. London, 1962.

"Readers and Writers," The *New Age*, new series, xxxi, nos. 10 (July 6, 1922), 11 (July 13, 1922), 12 (July 20, 1922), 13 (July 27, 1922), 14 (August 3, 1922), 15 (August 10, 1922), 16 (August 17, 1922), 17 (August 24, 1922), 18 (August 31, 1922), 19 (September 7, 1922), 21 (September 21, 1922).

Rustic Elegies. London, 1917.

The Shadow of Cain. London, 1947.

The Song of the Cold. New York, 1948 and London, 1945. The contents of the two editions differ.

The Sleeping Beauty. London, 1924.

Street Songs. London, 1942.

Taken Care Of. New York, 1965.

Trio, Dissertations on Some Aspects of National Genius. London, 1938. (With Osbert and Sacheverell Sitwell)

Troy Park, London, 1925.

Twentieth Century Harlequinade. Oxford, 1916. (With Osbert Sitwell)

The Wooden Pegasus. Oxford, 1920.

ANTHOLOGIES EDITED BY EDITH SITWELL

The American Genius. London, 1951.

The Atlantic Book of British and American Poetry. 2 vols. Boston, 1958.

A Book of Flowers. London, 1952.

A Book of the Winter. London, 1950.

Planet and Glow-Worm. London, 1944.

The Pleasures of Poetry. London, 1930 (First Series), 1931 (Second Series), 1932 (Third Series). Combined edition, 1934.

Swinburne. New York, 1960.

Wheels. Oxford, 1916 (First Cycle), 1917 (Second Cycle), 1918 (Third Cycle), 1919 (Fourth Cycle). London, 1920 (Fifth Cycle), 1921 (Sixth Cycle).